DAY TRADING GUIDE

Create a Passive Income Stream in 17 Days by Mastering Day Trading. Learn All the Strategies and Tools for Money Management, Discipline, and Trader Psychology
(2022 for Beginners)

Dwight Brown

TABLE OF CONTENTS

INTRODUCTION

Before the invention of computers, only those with direct access to stock exchanges were involved in trading.

The majority of these came from financial institutions, trading houses, or brokerage firms. Short-term trading was regarded as gambling; day trading was not popular at the time, and stock markets were only for long-term investing.

When the internet became widely available to the general public, day trading or short-term trading grew in popularity. Online trading and brokerage firms arose quickly and drew a large customer base. The ease of accessing stock markets from one's home or while sitting in a cafe created a new and lucrative career for those interested in financial markets. Suddenly, the term "investor" became archaic, while "day trading" became fashionable.

Some misconceptions arose as a result of the growing popularity and concept of making money by simply sitting at a desk. Before delving deeper into the mechanism of daily trading, we must dispel these myths.

Day trading is NOT a quick-money scheme:

The most enticing aspect of day trading, as well as the most common misconception, is that it is a money-making machine. It is not the case. People mistakenly believe that all you have to do is buy and sell every day to make a lot of money. This type of thinking leads to massive losses for retail traders who enter the stock market blindly, listen to the advice of their friends, colleagues, TV experts, or even seamstresses, and eventually, lose their shirts. Trading in financial markets necessitates a thorough understanding of how these entities work, as well as a disciplined approach and a great deal of patience. Make the mistake of thinking of day trading as simple as playing the lottery or gambling in casinos. Making money in any business does not rely on luck or chance. It is a calculated risk that is taken after thorough research and knowledge of that field of business. If you want to enter the world of day trading, make it your career, and make a living from it, you must first learn its intricacies. Examine all of the factors that influence day trading results. Take a step-by-step approach to acquire the skill sets required to become a successful day trader.

After all, if you're spending money to make money, you can't afford to fail in that endeavor.

Day trading is NOT a nine-to-five job:

Another common misunderstanding that leads to losses for many retail traders is that day trading is similar to their 9-to-5 job. They assume that you begin trading as soon as markets open (by arriving at work at a specific time), trade throughout the day, and close your trades when the closing bell rings (leave the work workplace at a fixed hour).

The operation of financial markets is not like a regular desk job. A variety of factors influence the operation of financial markets and their constituents, such as stocks, commodities, currencies, and indices.

These are all-day trading instruments that are influenced by business, finance, and geopolitical events. There is a very common trading term. It's referred to as "market volatility."

The fluctuation in financial markets is denoted by this term. While most 9-to-5 desk jobs have few "fluctuations" or rapid changes, in the world of trading, fluctuations happen in seconds! For new traders, this volatility can be stomach-churning. Only by understanding how markets work and learning to trade with volatility can one master these volatile fluctuations in stock markets. Remember that when you start day trading, you are putting your money at risk. Your goal should be to learn everything you can to reduce risk and increase your chances of success.

CHAPTER 1:

HOW DAY TRADING WORKS

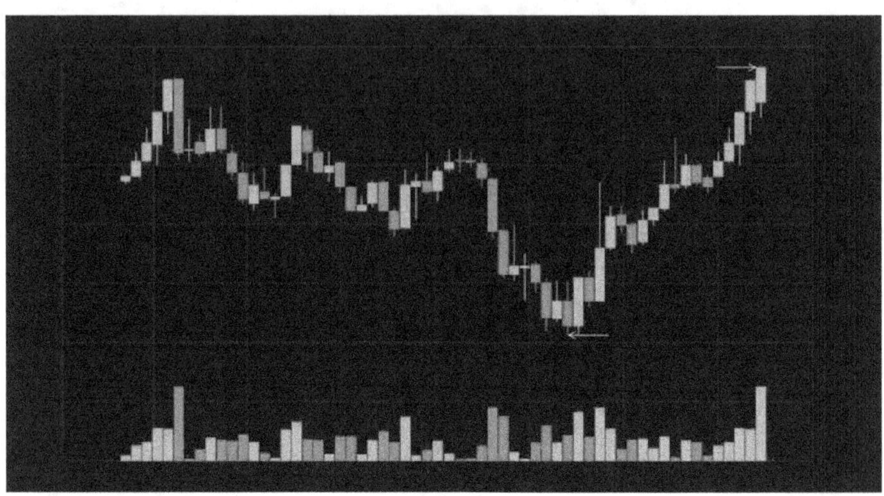

Always keep in mind the primary rule of day trading: never hold a position overnight, even if it means taking a loss on trades.

But why do you have to follow this rule even if it means losing money in the market? After all, isn't the goal of day trading to make money?

Yes, the goal of day trading is to make money. However, because the best securities for day trading are volatile, holding them overnight puts you at risk of suffering significant losses the next day. When you try to hold day trading securities overnight in the hopes that prices will recover significantly the next day, it's better to take small losses on day trades than large ones.

You can minimize day trading losses by closing your position at the end of the day, even if it is a loss. And if you can close positions at a profit, that's fantastic! Don't think you'll be able to earn more money if you wait until tomorrow. Remember, a bird in hand is worth three in the bush.

You should also keep in mind that trading is not the same as regular investing. While trading is a type of investing, regular investing is a more passive, buy-and-hold strategy that waits months or years before taking profits.

Trading has a much shorter time frame, which is only a couple of months at most for swing trading and several hours for day trading.

Investing in Long-Term Assets and Selling Short-Term Assets

When you purchase financial security, you are assuming a long position in that security. When a trader says he or she is long 100 shares of Intel stock, it means that the trader has purchased and is currently holding a hundred shares of Intel stock. The purpose of taking a long position in financial security is to sell it later at a higher price.

To close a long position, you sell the securities that you own.

When you sell securities that you do not yet own, you are taking a short position in those securities. When a trader says he or she shorted or sold short 100 shares of Intel stock, it means that the trader sold 100 shares of Intel stock in the hopes that the price will continue to fall so that he or she can repurchase it at a much lower price. It's the same concept as buying low and selling high, except the "selling high" part comes before the "buying low."

How can you sell something you don't have, and, more importantly, why would you?

First, let us discuss why you should do so. And the answer is: to profit when the value of securities falls. As previously stated, it is simply a reversal of the general trading strategy of purchasing securities at low prices and selling them at higher prices. You can trade profitably even during market downturns by selling securities at high prices and buying them later at lower prices.

How are you going to do it now? You can borrow securities from your broker, sell them, repurchase them when prices fall, and return the securities you borrowed from your broker, depending on your broker and whether you are qualified. You profit from the short sale in the process.

Keep in mind, however, that short selling, like long positions, has risks, including the possibility that prices will rise instead of continuing to fall. You may also incur trading losses in this case.

You might be wondering why brokers or exchanges would lend securities to their clients for short selling rather than sell the securities themselves. That's a great question. And the answer is that brokers are typically interested in taking long-term positions on securities.

Why?

Why take risks with short-term trades in a down trending market when they can make much more money by simply lending it to customers who want to short sell for a fee? Everyone benefits in this manner. Long-term investors can keep their securities and profit even during bear markets, whereas those who do not own securities can make profitable trades through short selling.

Retail Traders vs. Institutional Investors

Retail traders are individuals who trade on a part-time or full-time basis but do not work for a firm and do not manage funds from other people. These traders control a small portion of the trade market's volume.

Institutional traders, on the other hand, are made up of hedge funds, mutual funds, and investment banks that are often armed with advanced software and typically engage in high-frequency trading.

Human involvement in the operations of investment firms is now quite limited. Institutional investors, backed by professional analysts and large investments, can be quite aggressive.

So, at this point, you may be wondering how a newcomer like you can compete with the big boys.

Our benefit is the freedom and flexibility we have. Institutional traders are required by law to trade. Individual traders, in the meantime, are free to trade or refrain from trading if the market is currently volatile.

Regardless of the stock price, institutional traders should be active in the market and trade large volumes of stocks. Individual traders are free to sit out and trade if opportunities arise in the market.

Unfortunately, most retail traders lack the knowledge to determine when it is best to be active and when it is best to wait. To be profitable in day trading, you must overcome greed and cultivate patience.

The biggest issue with day traders is not the size of their accounts or a lack of access to technology, but rather a lack of discipline. Many people are prone to poor money management and excessive trading.

Some retail traders are successful by employing the guerilla strategy, which refers to the unconventional trading approach derived from guerilla warfare. Guerilla combatants are skilled at manipulating a more visible and less mobile conventional opponent through hit-and-run tactics such as raids, sabotage, and ambushes.

Keep in mind that your goal is not to defeat institutional traders.

Instead, concentrate on waiting for the right opportunity to earn your desired income.

You can profit from market volatility as a retail trader. When the markets are flat, it can be difficult to make money. Only institutional traders have the resources, expertise, and capital to gamble in such situations.

You must learn how to select stocks that will allow you to make quick decisions to the downside or upside in a predictable manner. Institutional traders, on the other hand, practice high-frequency trading, which allows them to profit from minor price movements.

But, in a nutshell, Alpha Predators are what retail traders are looking for. These stocks typically tank when the markets are rising and rise when the markets are falling.

It is generally acceptable if the market and the stocks are both running. Just make sure you're trading stocks that are moving because they have a valid reason to move and aren't simply reacting to market conditions.

You're probably wondering what the necessary catalyst for stocks is for them to be suitable for day trading.

Here are some examples of catalysts:

- Debt sacrifices
- Buybacks
- Splitting of stocks
- Management shifts
- Layoffs
- Restructuring
- Contract wins/losses that are significant
- Partnerships/alliances
- Important product launches
- Acquisitions and/or mergers
- FDA approval/rejection
- Surprising earnings
- Earnings statements

Retail traders who engage in reversal trades typically select stocks that are selling off as a result of negative press about the company. When there is a rapid sell-off due to negative press, many traders will notice and begin monitoring the stock for what is known as a bottom reversal.

How can you spot the stocks that are enticing retail investors? There are some tried-and-true methods for accomplishing this.

To begin, you can employ day trading stock scanners. Retail traders are primarily interested in stocks that are significantly moving up or down at price.

Second, look for online community groups or social media groups for retail traders. Twitter and Stock Twits are frequently good places to learn about current trends. If you follow successful traders regularly, you will be able to see for yourself what everyone is following.

Being a part of a day trading community has a significant advantage.

Securities at Risk

There's a reason why so many investors, traders, and analysts pay attention to market movements or indices. It's because they understand that, for the most part, most financial securities will follow the overall trend of their respective markets unless they have compelling reasons to do otherwise. For example, when the Dow Jones is trending upward, the prices of most NYSE stocks tend to rise, and vice versa.

However, there will always be outliers who, for one reason or another, will deviate from the general trend for a specific reason.

They are picking up when their general markets are tanking. When the rest of the world's markets are improving, theirs is tanking.

These are known as securities in play (SIP). These are the securities you should concentrate on as a retail or individual day trader in your chosen day trading market.

These are stocks to day trade if you want to deviate from the general trend of the NYSE or NASDAQ. If futures contracts are used, they will be against the general direction of most other similar agreements.

You get the idea, don't you? Right!

What are some of the possible explanations for SIPs' contrarian behavior? These could include:

Unexpected earnings results; Surprising company or economic developments; and Significant policy changes by the governing authorities.

So, just because security deviates from the general market trend does not imply that it is a SIP. The contrarian movement should be motivated by something. If there are none, it is most likely not a SIP.

Another important day trading rule to remember, especially when selecting SIPs to day trade: Determine whether the movement of a specific security is due to general market sentiment or a unique fundamental reason.

You'll need to do your homework for this. As a beginner day trader, you may need to do a little more research than usual. However, as you gain experience as a day trader, you'll be able to tell when security is simply following the general market trend and when it's trending for a unique and specific reason. Professional day traders are those who make a living from this type of trading. While other types of trading can be done as a hobby or to get a gambling high, day trading is frequently excluded. You will most likely lose money if you do not understand the market and its fundamentals.

CHAPTER 2:

HOW TO THINK LIKE AN EXPERT TRADER

Know when to deviate from the plan: While sticking to your plan, even when your emotions tell you to ignore it, is a sign of a successful trader, this does not imply that you must blindly follow your plan 100 percent of the time. You will, without a doubt, find yourself in a situation where your plan is rendered completely useless by something beyond your control from time to time. You must be aware of your plan's flaws as well as changing market conditions to recognize that following your predetermined course of action will result in failure rather than success. Knowing when the situation is truly changing versus when your emotions are trying to take control is something that takes practice, but even being aware of the difference is a huge step in the right direction.

Trades that are out of the money should be avoided: While there are a few strategies out there that make a point of purchasing options that are currently out of stock, you can rest assured that they are the exception rather than the rule. Remember that the options market is not the same as the traditional stock market, which means that even if you are trading options based on underlying stocks, buying low and selling high is simply not a viable strategy. If a call has dropped out of the money, there is generally less than a 10% chance that it will return to acceptable levels before it expires, which means that purchasing these types of options is little better than gambling, and there are ways to gamble with odds much higher than 10% in your favor.

Avoid clinging to your initial strategy too tightly: That does not, however, imply that it is the last strategy you will ever require. Your core trading strategy should always be changing and evolving as the circumstances surrounding your trading habits change and evolve. Furthermore, in addition to your primary strategy, you will want to develop additional plans that are more specifically tailored to various market states or specific strategies that are only useful in a narrow range of situations. Remember, the more prepared you are before beginning a trading day, the higher your overall profit level is likely to be; it's as simple as that.

Make use of the spread: If you are not completely risk-averse, then when it comes to taking advantage of volatile trades, the best thing to do is use a spread as a way of both protecting your existing investments and making a profit. To use a long spread, create a call and a put with the same underlying asset, expiration details, and share amounts but two drastically different strike prices. The call must have a higher strike price to represent the upper limit of your profits, while the put must have a lower strike price to represent the lower limit of your losses. When creating a spread, it is critical to purchase both halves at the same time, as doing so in fits and spurts can introduce extraneous variables into the formula that are difficult to adjust properly. Never proceed without first ascertaining the market's mood: While using a personalized trading plan is always the best option, having one does not change the fact that it is critical to consider the market's mood before proceeding with the day's trades. First and foremost, it is critical to remember that the collective will of all traders currently participating in the market is just as powerful as anything more concrete, such as market news. Even if companies release good news to various outlets and the news isn't quite as good as everyone expected, related prices can still fall.

To get a good sense of the market's current mood, you should be aware of the average daily numbers that are common in your market and keep an eye out for them to begin dropping sharply. While a day or two of major fluctuation is normal, anything more than that is a sure sign that something is wrong. Furthermore, you should always be aware of what the major players in your market are up to.

Never begin without a clear entry and exit strategy: While determining your first set of entry/exit points without experience can be difficult, you must have them nailed down before you begin trading, even if the stakes are low. Unless you are extremely lucky, starting without a clear understanding of the playing field will result in you losing money. If you're not sure what limits to set, start with a generalized pair of points and work your way up from there.

More important than establishing entry and exit points, however, is using them even when there appears to be money on the table.

One of the most difficult obstacles for new options traders to overcome is the belief that you must squeeze every last penny out of every successful trade. The truth is that as long as you have a profitable trading strategy, there will always be more profitable trades in the future, which means that rather than worrying about a small extra profit, you should be more concerned with protecting the profit that the trade has already netted you. While ignoring this advice may occasionally result in a small profit, the chances are that you will lose far more than you gain as profits peak unexpectedly and begin to fall again before you can effectively pull the trigger.

If you're still having trouble grasping this concept, consider this:

Options trading is a marathon, not a sprint; slow and steady wins the race every time.

17

Never, ever double down: Many new options traders will find themselves in a situation where the best way to recoup a significant loss is to double down on the underlying stock in question at its newest, significantly lowered, price in an attempt to make a profit under the assumption that things will turn around and then continue to do so until everything is completely profitable once again. While it can be difficult to let go of an underlying stock that was once extremely profitable, doubling down is rarely, if ever, the right decision.

If you find yourself in a situation where you are unsure whether the trade you are about to make is a good one, simply ask yourself if you would make the same one if you were going into the situation blind. The answer should tell you everything you need to know. If you find yourself in a situation where doubling down appears to be the best option, you will need the strength to talk yourself back down from that investing ledge and to cut your losses as thoroughly as possible given the current situation.

The sooner you cut your losses and move on from a losing trade, the sooner you can start putting your energy and investments into a trade that still has the potential to profit you.

Nothing should ever be taken personally: It is human nature to construct stories around, and thus form relationships with, inanimate objects such as individual stocks or currency pairs. This is why it is perfectly natural to develop a stronger attachment to specific trades and even consider abandoning your strategy if one of them takes an unexpected dive. However, thinking about and acting are two very different things, which is why being aware of these tendencies is essential to avoid them at all costs.

This scenario occurs just as frequently with positive trades as it does with negative trades, but the results are always the same. In particular, it can be extremely tempting to hold on to a given trade for much longer than you might otherwise decide to do simply because it is on a hot streak that shows no signs of abating. In these cases, the better course of action is to sell half of your shares and then set a new target based on the updated information to ensure you can have your cake and eat it too.

Not taking your broker's recommendation seriously: With so many factors to consider, it's easy to see why many new option traders simply choose the first broker they come across and start trading from there. The fact of the matter is, however, that the broker you choose will be a significant part of your overall trading experience, which means that the importance of selecting the right one should not be underestimated if you want to have the best experience possible. This means that the first thing you should do is look past the friendly exterior of their website and get to the meat and potatoes of what they truly offer.

Remember that while creating an eye-catching website is simple, filling it with legitimate information while having malicious intent is much more difficult.

First and foremost, this entails investigating their customer service history to ensure not only that they treat their customers properly, but also that the quality of service is where it should be. Remember that when you make a trade, every second counts, so if you need to contact your broker for assistance with a trade, you need to know that you will be speaking with someone who can solve your problem as soon as possible. Giving them a call and seeing how long it takes for them to get back to you is the best way to ensure their customer service is up to par. If you wait more than one business day, take your business elsewhere because if they are this uninterested in a new client, imagine what the service will be like when they already have you right where they want you.

With that out of the way, the next thing you'll need to think about is the fees that the broker will charge for their services.

When it comes to these fees, there is very little regulation, which means it will pay to shop around. In addition to fees, it is critical to consider any required account minimums as well as any fees associated with withdrawing funds from the account.

Locate a Mentor: When it comes to progressing from a casual trader to someone who trades successfully regularly, there is only so much you can learn on your own before you need a truly objective eye to ensure you are on the right track.

This person could be someone you know in person, or it could be one or more people you've met online. The point is that you need to find another person or two with whom you can bounce ideas and benefit from their experience. Options trading does not have to be a solitary activity; join any community you can find.

CHAPTER 3:

GETTING READY FOR YOUR DAY TRADING CAREER

Welcome to the start of the rest of your life. This is the chapter in which we discuss how to prepare your life for becoming a day trader, organizing everything you need to get off to the best possible start. This will be a long chapter because there is a lot to cover, such as determining whether you're cut out to be a trader, setting up your trading space, organizing your finances, and getting ready to go. Let's get started.

Is Day Trading a Good Option for You?

This is a critical question you must ask yourself.

Using the questions outlined above, you must ensure that you are committed to becoming a day trader. You must understand that you will be working long hours, and you will not receive holiday breaks because you are your boss and work for yourself. You must also ensure that you are not an emotionally reactive person. It is almost certain that you will invest in a stock at some point during your career and lose money on it.

That's just how the game is, and it's unavoidable. If, on the other hand, you're an emotional person and you lose a significant investment sum that causes you to freak out, you can bet you'll make some poor decisions in the future. Similarly, there will be times when you win big money, and it's natural to get excited and want to invest more and make more. This is known as greed, and it can have the same negative consequences.

Being a day trader entails remaining calm and relaxed in even the most stressful situations, removing emotion from decision-making, sticking to your plan, and remaining grounded. If you are not this type of person, or if you are unable to cultivate this mindset, then day trading is probably not for you.

Establishing Your Financial Situation

Before you enter the world of day trading, you must be able to manage your finances. If you are currently in debt, you should not even consider day trading until you have paid it off. If you have a loan or a credit card with a 20% interest rate and only a 5% return on your investments, you will lose money.

Instead, make sure you pay off all of your debts before preparing your capital. This way, you'll be minimizing the amount of interest you pay on credit and debt while maximizing your profits when you start investing.

When you're in the black, it's time to start thinking about raising capital. This is the initial amount of money you will invest with. This can vary greatly depending on your circumstances, so it's entirely up to you. You could begin with a small investment, such as $5,000, and then day trade part-time. As your capital grows, you can gradually transition to becoming a full-time trader.

On the other hand, you may want to save up a lump sum so that you can quit your job and begin investing right away, though this is not advised because you will have no experience. Even if you have a large sum of money, start small so you can learn the ins and outs of trading, and then gradually increase your investment as you gain experience.

Van Tharp, one of the world's top day traders and author of Trade Your Way to Financial Freedom, suggests that if you want to trade full-time, you should start with around $100,000.

If you want to day trade effectively, you'll need at least $10,000 in your trading account at all times.

The final financial aspect to consider is setting up a rainy-day emergency fund. This entails setting up a savings account in which you deposit a recommended three months' worth of living expenses and then leave it alone.

This means that when you're trading, and if you ever find yourself in a situation where you're experiencing financial difficulties, you'll have this fund to fall back on. However, you must keep in mind that this is not a trading or investment account. You don't want to end up with anything if you have a hard-losing streak and need money to support yourself and your family. This is a financial crisis you will want to avoid at all costs, so be as prepared as possible.

Discover More About Stock Market Trading

This should go without saying, but if you want to become a day trader, you must have a strong interest in the stock market, or at the very least the desire to learn more about it. You must learn when the stock market is open for business and how the stock market's processes and systems operate.

You should have an interest in the niche or industry you want to trade in, and you should be passionate about it because you'll need to be watching the news on this industry, reading articles and books on the subject, and investing your time watching interviews and learning about these stock market companies in terms of how they work and what they're up to daily. You'll also need to learn about stocks and other potential trading options like ETFs, options, futures, and mutual funds.

We'll go over each one briefly in the table below, but you must take the time to understand each one before you start implementing and investing in one.

Stocks When a company's or organization's ownership is divided into individual shares, these are referred to as "stocks." Each stock represents fractional ownership of a company about the total number of shares it owns.

ETFs is an abbreviation for 'Exchange-Traded Funds.' ETFs are a type of investment fund that trades exactly like a stock on the world's stock exchanges. ETFs are indexes that are composed of other securities and assets, such as stocks, special funds, and commodity funds.

The term "options" refers to a contract that grants a specific buyer the right to buy or sell any underlying asset, but it does not guarantee a sale obligation. Options, on the other hand, will provide a price that must be valid before or on a specified date specified on the option contract.

Futures are another type of contract that refers to a legal agreement that contracts the buying and selling of something at a predetermined price, time, and date. These metrics, however, will not be known by the parties involved and are classified as an asset.

Investing in Mutual Funds Mutual funds are investment portfolios managed by professionals in the financial services industry. These services collect funds from a variety of investors to purchase stocks, shares, and other securities such as those listed in this table.

Precious metals and gold Gold (and sometimes other precious metals) refers to the metal gold's trading asset that is stored in banks throughout the United States and around the world.

Eminis are a type of futures contract that follows the S&P 500 stock index market. It is also referred to as the E-Mini, ES, or simply Mini.

Cryptocurrencies This is a broad term for the trading of cryptocurrencies on the stock market. This can be done either individually or through an exchange.

Forex refers to the global trading of foreign currencies by converting one currency into another and then continuing to trade in this manner.

Work on Your Money Management Skills

Before you even begin to consider getting ready to trade stocks, you should consider how effective your money management skills are. If you're thinking, 'yeah, my money management skills are pretty good,' take a step back and think about how you can improve. There is always room for improvement, and as a day trader, these are enhancements you will both want and require.

Consider the following. How much are you going to invest, to begin with, if you start with $100,000 and use a tried-and-tested strategy with a 60% success rate? What if your first four trades fail and result in a loss? What should you do with your money?

When it comes to trading, it's always a good idea to start small and then grow over time. It's a bad idea to make your first trade by buying $100,000 worth of stock and hoping for the best. Of course, it could pay off, but if you're this reckless with your first investment, chances are it'll backfire spectacularly later on. Instead, work on your money management skills and cultivate the ability to step back and make decisions from a grounded state of mind. You must be able to make sound decisions about which opportunities to pursue and how to manage your investment capital.

Even if you use a strategy that has a 30% success rate, you can still make a significant profit if you have good money management skills.

You're one step closer to starting your day trading career once you've developed all of these aspects of your life and prepared yourself. Before we get into the meat of what you need to do and start investing, there's one more thing we need to talk about: developing your day trading mindset.

What Motivates You to Trade?

The answer is straightforward: the only reason to trade is to make money! This question, "Why do you trade?" is important to consider as we wrap up this topic. While the answer "to make money" may appear obvious, most losing traders trade for other reasons. They may believe they are trading for profit, but their actions suggest that other motivations are driving their decisions. Remember that you are the most important indicator.

If you are trading to make money, the next logical question is how... How does a trader achieve that goal? Trading within the context and rules of a proven trade plan is the answer. Despite the random distribution of wins and losses, a proven trade plan increases equity in your account. It contains rules to follow that you can demonstrate to yourself.

Taking random trades that are not part of a proven trading strategy is not trading to make money. It's something else entirely. Why?

We are traders, after all. That's what we do. We accept trades. What happens if you win a random trade? Isn't there still another trade to be made? Making money comes from the advantage that your tried-and-true trading strategy provides you over time. Random trades will not reveal whether or not you have an edge—they are random—until after the fact, when you will almost certainly discover that the answer is no, you did not have an edge. And by that time, it will be too late. This is how accounts are destroyed.

If you truly want to make money trading, your actions should reflect that. If they don't, you're most likely trading for reasons you don't fully comprehend. If you truly want to internalize the correct reason to trade— to make money—you must address this. Otherwise, the market will provide you with something else, which you will most likely dislike.

CHAPTER 4:

RISK AND ACCOUNT MANAGEMENT

Because the goal of every good trader is to make a profit, to be a good and successful trader, you must learn how to manage trading risks and protect your profits.

How well you manage your risks determines your level of success as a trader.

Prepare your mind, because you are about to learn simple but powerful and practical risk management strategies and techniques.

Making a Trade Plan

Sun Tzu, a Chinese military general, once said, "Every battle is won before it is fought," implying that planning and strategy are critical in trading. It is unavoidable to plan. "Plan the trade and trade the plan," as the famous saying goes. This determines the success or failure of your trade; no successful trader enters the trade without carefully planning it out, pointing out potential future losses, calculating risks, and listing potential future profits in your trade. A plan should be written clearly and concisely; your plan should be adaptable to market changes, and risk tolerance should be considered. Here are some steps you must take to have a successful trade plan:

Skill Assessment: You should be able to assess yourself very well here to determine how prepared you are to trade. You should ask yourself a critical question, such as "Are you ready to trade?"

How confident are you in a particular market? Have you put your system to the test by trading on paper? (Paper trading is a method of practicing buying and selling without using real money; it is typically done through online trading platforms such as paper Money and Investopedia.) How confident are you that your system will function properly in a live trading environment? Can you detect and follow your signals without wasting time? Mental prepping: As a good trader, you should be emotionally and mentally prepared for the upcoming tasks, as well as prepared for any situation that may arise and changes in your market. Avoid distractions in your trading area as much as possible. If you are emotionally incapable, try taking a day off, resting, and exercising.

This prepares your brain for the upcoming task because trading requires a lot of thinking.

Also, before the day begins, have a market mantra; this is a special quote or phrase that prepares you for trading. Set your risk level: this is how much of your portfolio you should risk on a trade. All financial assets, such as bonds, stocks, and currencies, as well as cash, commodities, and cash equivalents, are included in your portfolio.

This is determined by how you trade and your risk tolerance; it can vary, but it should be between 1% and 5% of your portfolio on any given trading day. If you lose any of that money in a single day, exit the market and save your portfolio for a better market.

Consider the One-Percentage-Point Rule.

The one-percent rule is used by most successful traders; it simply states that you should never invest more than one percent of your capital or portfolio in a single trade or market. This means that if you have $10,000 in your trading account, the most you should invest in a single trade should not be more than $100. Traders with less than $100,000 in their accounts are most likely to use this technique. Some other traders may choose to go as high as 2%. Everything is dependent on your position and the size of your account. The best thing to do is to keep the rule at or below 2%.

Defining Stop-Loss and Profit Levels

A stop-loss point occurs when a trader decides to sell a stock and bear the loss, as the name implies. This situation usually occurs when the market does not turn out well enough for the trader.

The stock's value in the market falls far below expectations, so the trader decides to sell it before it falls any further.

The take profit point is the price at which a trader will sell a stock for a profit. Traders typically sell before a period of consolidation occurs.

How to Set Stop-Loss Points More Effectively

Technical analysis is typically used to set stop-loss points to profit, though fundamental analysis can assist. Resistance trend lines are a great way to set stop-loss or take-profit levels; they can be created by connecting and comparing previous highs and lows.

Diversify and hedge your bets

Diversification and hedging are synonymous with the adage "never put all your eggs in one basket." You are taking a significant risk if you choose to invest all of your money in one stock. As a result, diversify your investments across industries. There may also be times when you need to hedge at a specific position based on the stock and the market.

In conclusion

You should be able to tell when to enter or exit a trade as a good trader. The trader can reduce losses by using a stop-loss order. It is preferable to plan ahead of time.

Calculating Expected Returns

Calculating expected returns is critical in risk management because it helps you think through your trade and is an excellent way to compare trades to select the most profitable and least risky ones. Returns can be calculated as follows:

[(Probability of Gain) (Take Profit Percentage Gain)] + [(Probability of Loss) (Stop Loss Percentage Loss)]

The result should be the expected returns.

Day Trading Dangers

To be a successful trader, you must be aware of the various risks that you will face before entering the trading world.

There are three major risk categories:

Market Dangers

Understanding market changes in your trade are critical to the success of your business. Understanding when the markets rise and fall, as well as the potential risks associated with them, will allow you to better protect your profits. Market risks include the following: Inflation risk: When there is uncertainty about the future value of an investment, inflation occurs. While deflation may result in increased returns and profit for you. Rising inflation frequently reduces the expected returns and profit. This also implies that as the price of stocks and commodities rises, so does the demand for them. As a result, you should prepare your strategy for any market changes.

Marketability risk indicates how easily your investment can be sold. If there is any resistance or delay in effectively selling or marketing your investment, your target market will be meaningless.

For example, if you choose to invest in a small company whose stock isn't traded on one of the major stock exchanges, you risk losing your money. Currency translation risk occurs when there are fluctuations in the values of your local currency and the currency of your international trading country when you trade with foreign countries. Currency trading risk knowledge would be very beneficial to traders because even if your stock or investment rises in price, you can still lose money depending on the currency exchange rate between the two countries. If the value of your local currency falls against the value of the other currency, your investment may be much smaller when converted back.

Investing Dangers

This refers to how you invest your money and manage it when you enter or exit trades. There are two types of risks:

Opportunity risks: This type of investment risk prevents you from investing in other more profitable trades because your money is already invested in your current business. This type of risk causes you to miss out on golden opportunities because your money is being held hostage by another.

Concentration risks occur when you concentrate all of your investment and capital on just one trade, possibly because you believe you have discovered your dream trade that will make you a millionaire. As a result, you invest everything you have, leaving yourself extremely vulnerable to any potential risks that may arise in that trade, with the possibility of losing it all.

Trading Dangers

Trading risks are common risks that swing traders face, and every trader should be aware of them. As the saying goes, "knowledge is power," and being aware of them will give you leverage in managing future risks that may arise. Some of the most common risks associated with trading risks are as follows:

Slippage risk: This risk draws attention to some hidden costs that may be associated with each transaction made by the trader. Every time you enter or exit a trade, a very minor and insignificant amount of money is deducted from your account. Also, if you buy a stock at the asking price, which is the lowest price available for the stock you want, and sells it at the bid price, which is the highest price someone is willing to pay for your shares, you must be aware that the bid price is always less than the asking price. The amount for each trade may appear small at first, but as your trading increases, so do your losses.

Poor execution risk: this risk occurs when your broker has difficulty filling your order, possibly due to fast market conditions, insufficient stock availability, or the absence of other buyers and sellers. When this occurs, you risk having your stock trade go lower than expected or not having your order filled at all.

Gap risk occurs when there are price gaps in your transactions; a stock may open at a significantly higher or lower price and may trade using your exit price. For example, a stock may close today at $35 and open tomorrow at $30. If your planned price is $34, your order will almost certainly be filled at the opening price.

Though these types of risks are uncommon, they can cause issues for most traders.

Risks of Other Kinds Include

BLACK SWAN EVENTS: These are risks that appear unexpectedly. They are difficult to forecast. It is a type of significant risk with a significant impact on the market.

UNDIVERSIFIED RISK: This is a risk that occurs when you "put all your eggs in one basket." This type of risk is typically difficult to avoid and predict, as markets can also influence this type of risk. This is one of the primary reasons why investors and traders choose to diversify their stocks and money to avoid the risk of losing everything all at once.

CHAPTER 5:

PSYCHOLOGY DISCIPLINE

Emotional Investing

When day trading, it is common for traders to have their emotions and feelings jumbled up as a result of the market's highs and lows. This is a far cry from the confident self that a trader usually portrays before the markets open, brimming with anticipation of the money and profits that they intend to make.

Emotions in trading can cloud your judgment and impair your ability to make sound decisions. Day trading should not be done without emotion, but rather as a trader. You should be able to work your way around them and make them work for you. A clear, level-headed, and stable mind should be maintained at all times, whether your profits are increasing or you are on a losing streak. This is not to say that you should disconnect from your emotions as a trader.

Greed

A trader may be motivated to earn more money after checking their account balances and discovering that it is at a low level. While this may be a motivator to work hard, some traders take it too far, expecting to earn a large sum of money right away. They make mistakes in trading that have the opposite effect of what they intended...

Unnecessary Risk-Taking

Greed for more money will try to persuade the trader to take unnecessary risks in order to reach a certain financial threshold in the trading account. These will almost certainly result in losses. Risky traders may take risks such as high leverage, which they hope will work in their favor but may result in massive losses.

Performing an Overtrade

A trader may trade for extended periods of time due to the desire to make more and more money. Often, these efforts are futile, because overtrading through market highs and lows puts a trader in a position where their accounts can be wiped out as a result of greed. Not taking into account the time of trading and rushing into opening trades without first conducting an analysis will almost certainly result in a loss.

Inadequate Profit and Loss Understanding

Wanting to make a lot of money in a short period of time will cause a trader to not close a losing trade, keeping the losses, and on the other hand, overriding on a profitable trade until the market reverses, canceling out all the gains made.

Fear

Fear can act in both directions, as a limit to over-trading and as a limit to profit-making. A trader may close a trade in order to avoid a loss, which is motivated by fear. A trader may also close a trade too soon, even if it is on a winning streak, in fear that the market will reverse and result in losses. Fear is the motivator in both scenarios, working to avoid both failure and success.

The Fear of Failure

The fear of losing money in trading may prevent a trader from opening trades and simply watching the market change and move in cycles while doing nothing. The fear of losing money in trading is a deterrent to success. It prevents a trader from carrying out what could have been a profitable transaction.

The Fear of Success

This type of fear in trading psychology will cause a trader to give up profits to the market when there is an opportunity to do so.

In market scenarios, it has a self-destructive effect. Such traders in this category are afraid of making too much profit and allow losses to run, despite being aware of their activities and the losses they will incur.

Trading Dishonesty

There are several market biases that a trader may develop as a result of emotional play, which traders should avoid.

These biases in trading psychology may influence a trader to make unwise and uncalculated trading decisions that may prove to be loss-making. Even when your trading biases are in focus, you must be aware of your emotions as a trader and devise ways to keep them in check while maintaining a cool head in your trading window.

Overconfidence Bias

It is common for traders, especially new traders, to experience euphoria in the state of winning after making a large profit on a trade. You want to keep opening trades with the conviction that your analysis can't go wrong, all the way down to the profits and gains you've made.

This should not be happening. You can't be so excited and confident in your analysis skills that you believe you can't lose. Because the market is volatile, the cards can change at any time, and when they do, the over-excited and overconfident trader becomes a disappointing one.

Bias in Trade Confirmation

In trading psychology, one of the factors that wastes a lot of time and money for traders is the bias in confirmation of a trade you have already made, justifying it. Professional traders are more likely to exhibit this type of bias. They return to evaluate and analyze the trade they just made, attempting to prove that it was the correct one, whether they sailed according to the market.

They squander a lot of time digging for information that they already know. They could also be demonstrating that the mistake they made in opening a bad trade and making a bad move was correct.

Anchoring on Obsolete Strategies Leads to Bias

This type of bias in trading psychology applies to traders who rely on outdated information and strategies that do more harm than good to their trading success.

Anchoring on correct but irrelevant information when trading may expose the trader to losses, which is a setback for traders who are always too lazy to look for new market information. One of the most important aspects of having a successful trading career is keeping up with current events and factors that may have an impact on the market.

Bias in Loss Avoidance

Trading for the purpose of avoiding losses usually boils down to the fear factor. Some traders' trading patterns and trading windows are dictated by their fear of losing money. Gains and profits are not motivators for them when fear prevents them from opening trades that could have been profitable. They also close trades too soon, even when they are profitable, in order to avoid their imaginable losses.

Traders' Habits Are Influenced by Psychology

A trader's trading habits, mistakes, and winning strategies are all influenced by psychological factors. The following are the negative habits that many traders develop as a result of the influence of psychology on their habits.

Trading Without a Plan

A trader will face difficulties if he or she does not have a trading strategy and plan to refer to. A trader should develop a proper strategy to use as a reference point when dealing with a problem in the market. It should be a well-thought-out plan that outlines what to do in specific situations and which trading patterns to employ in various case scenarios. Trading without a strategy is the same as trading to lose money.

Inadequate Financial Management Plans

Money management plans are one of the most important aspects of trading, and without solid strategies in this area, it is difficult to make progress in making profits on trades opened. As a trader, you must follow certain principles that will guide you in how to spend your money in the account in opening trades and ensuring profits.

Desire to Be Always Correct

Some traders always trade against the market, expressing their desire for the market to behave in a certain way. They do not follow the market signal, but rather their own philosophy, not doing proper analysis and always wanting to be right.

RESOLVING THE CONSEQUENCES OF PSYCHOLOGICAL HABITS

Developing Specific Goals

Creating clear and concise trading goals and strategies assists a trader in having a vision of trading and not just doing it for the sake of trading. Writing down goals can also help a trader's confidence levels. Working with a well-rounded strategy is a profitable plan in the market.

Setting Up Trading Rules

Rules for traders are beneficial in ensuring trading discipline. As a trader, you should establish rules that govern when you start trading, when you close your trades, and whether or not you trade on a daily basis, or whatever your trading window is. Rules are the foundation of successful trading; they dictate when to close a losing trade and when to close a winning one.

Developing Financial Management Strategies

Creating money strategies is not enough; it is also necessary to put the strategies into action.

Money management strategies are critical in ensuring that a trader's profitability comes first, while also taking into account the risk of loss. Implement the money strategy to avoid trading haphazardly and with emotions.

CHAPTER 6:

BUILD YOUR WATCH LIST

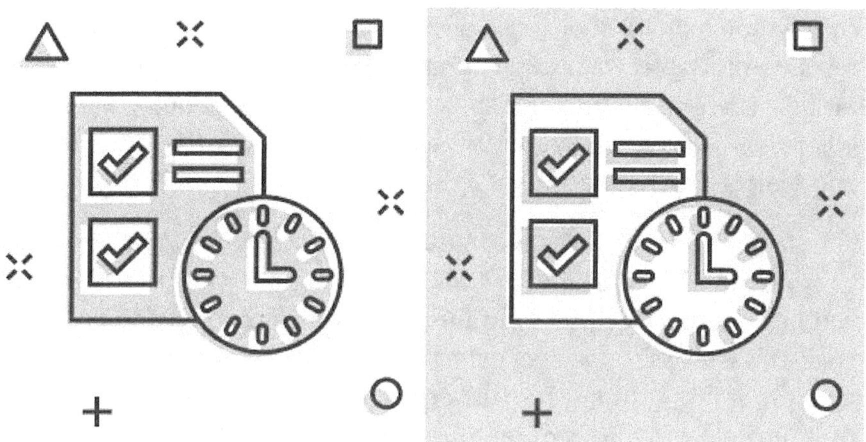

A Watch List for Trading

As a day trader, you must keep a trading watch list.

Essentially, this is a list in which you keep track of the daily share prices of a group of stocks over time. It functions as a trading day menu. A trading watch list should include active stocks that are ready to trade based on the fundamental and technical new catalyst. It can be completed on a notepad, a spreadsheet, or even on paper.

There are numerous software programs and other utilities available to assist in the creation of a watch list. It can also be provided by some brokerage houses for a small fee or for free.

A trader can have multiple watch lists, but there are two that every active trader should never mess with: a general watch list and a dynamic watch list. The general one could be made up of hundreds of stocks that the trader is familiar with. Every trader should also narrow down from the general watch list and create an active stock watch list before the market opens each trading day.

This watch list should include stocks that the trader has been monitoring for days or weeks and believe are about to set up for a technical move. The active trade list, unlike the general list, should not contain too many stocks. It should have a few ripe stocks that the trader feels comfortable trading. In other words, a general watch list may include shares that the trader has recently or previously purchased, whereas an active watch list should include stocks that the trader is considering purchasing.

Assume you are an active trader who holds ten positions on average at any given time. Typically, you will be tracking several stocks so that you can buy another position from the watch list as soon as one position is sold. This will assist you in avoiding a situation in which you have a large amount of idle cash in your trading account at any given time. A watch list is useful for a variety of reasons.

For example, suppose you've done your research and discovered a company that you believe is sound and has promising potential, but the stock price appears to be currently high or overvalued. You decide to postpone your purchase until a more convenient time comes along. The watch list will be used to track the stock price and generate charts to monitor the stock trends. That way, you'll be able to determine the best time to buy that stock.

CREATING A TRADING WATCH LIST

Stocks Under Consideration

A stock is said to be in play when it is widely believed to be a takeover target. Stocks in play are widely traded by day traders because their volatility generates reasonable risks and trading opportunities. When a company's stock has low volatility, it moves slowly and has a reasonable price change only when the company has good or bad trading results. This may happen only a few times a year. Such businesses are ideal for long-term investors seeking high returns. Long-term investors buy shares in these companies with good prospects, with shares moving slowly in the right direction, and it doesn't matter to them if the share price doesn't move much intraday. Day traders, on the other hand, buy and sell stocks during the stock market's opening hours and exit the trade before the day's end.

They may even trade for a few minutes or an hour before exiting the market. As a result, they require more action than investors. They require stocks that move and cause price swings for their trade to be profitable. Such price fluctuations allow them to profit after paying the association fees charged by stockbrokers for buying and selling shares.

Stocks in play have a high volume as well. Day traders are looking for quick entries and exits, as well as liquid stocks. That is, they can buy and sell stock shares on demand. A stock with low liquidity may take the broker longer to close a promising buying or selling transaction. The broker is unable to negotiate the trader's desired purchase or sale price. This is a problem for day traders because it can mean the difference between a profitable and non-profitable trade. Day traders are guided by the volume of shares traded each day to determine what they consider to be good liquidity for them. Most traders would consider 100,000 shares traded per day to be the bare minimum, while others may require a million shares.

The stocks in play will change in a single day. An ordinary stock will be put into play by company news, which is typically released early in the morning, and the price will vary depending on the nature of the news, whether it is good or bad.

Good news for traders isn't always bad news for investors.

Some of the largest companies, such as Apple, Amazon, and Facebook, have stocks that are constantly in play, and day traders will keep these stocks on their watch list at all times. This is due to the high volume of trades and traded shares. This is where a day trader looks for excellent trading opportunities and appropriate trading levels.

Other websites offer free stock screening tools to help traders find stocks that are moving quickly, intraday, or breaking out before the market opens. Market watch and busy stock are examples of such websites.

ADVFN generates breakout shares and top lists for trending UK stocks. They also have apps, such as Seeking Alpha, that provide you with live news feeds. News outlets such as CNN, BBC, Reuters, and Bloomberg provide timely coverage of major corporate announcements and breaking news. Channels such as Stock twits also provide up-to-the-minute news for day traders.

Float and Market Capitalization

As a day trader, it is critical to understand the relationship between company size, risk, and potential return. Such information is critical as you lay the groundwork for long-term trading objectives. With this knowledge, you can create a well-balanced watch list that includes companies with a variety of market capitalizations.

Market capitalization is referred to as market capitalization. It represents the total stock value of the company's shares. To calculate an entity's market cap, multiply its shares by its stock price.

If an entity has $50 million in shares and each share is worth $20, its market capitalization is $10 billion. Market capitalization is important because it allows traders to understand and compare the size of various companies. Market capitalization informs you of the value of various companies on the open market. It also assists you in understanding how the market perceives a specific company and reflects what investors and traders are willing to pay for its stock.

Large-cap stocks have a stock market value of $10 billion or more.

These are typically reputable businesses that produce high-quality goods and services. They have a track record of consistent dividend payments to shareholders and have experienced consistent growth. Their brand names are well-known among national and even international consumers. They are dominant players in the establishment's respective industries. They are ideal for conservative investors because they pose less risk and have less growth potential.

Mid-cap stocks: These are typically companies with a minimum market value of $2 billion and a maximum market value of $10 billion.

In other words, their market capitalization ranges between $2 billion and $10 billion. They are medium-sized, well-established businesses with room for expansion. Such businesses are experiencing rapid growth or are expected to grow rapidly shortly. They are in the process of increasing its competitive advantage and expanding its market share. This is a critical stage because it determines their ability to reach their full potential. In terms of risk, they are less risky than new businesses.

When it comes to potential, they outperform blue-chip companies because they are expected to grow until they reach their full potential.

Small caps have market capitalizations ranging from $300 million to $2 billion. They are expanding businesses that are new to the industry. They are the riskiest and most aggressive, relying on niche marketing to survive in the industry. They are vulnerable to economic shocks due to limited resources. They are vulnerable to intense competition and market volatility. Because they are new startups, they have high long-term growth potential, and they are ideal for investors who can tolerate volatile stock price swings in the short run.

The number of shares available for trading by the general public, on the other hand, is known as the float. Unlike market capitalization, which calculates the total stock value of all company shares, free float excludes locked-in shares. Employees of the company and the government own locked-in shares. Several factors can influence market capitalization. A significant change in the value of shares, either up or down, can affect the market cap. When the number of issued shares changes, the market cap can also change. When warrants on the company's stock are exercised, the number of shares outstanding increases, causing the market cap to be diluted. This is due to the fact that such an exercise is frequently performed below the market price of the shares, which has the potential to affect the market cap. A dividend or a stock split, on the other hand, usually does not affect the market cap.

To create a consistent watch list of large-cap, mid-cap, and small-cap stocks, a trader must consider their time horizon, risk tolerance, and financial goals. A well-balanced watch list that includes all market caps may be ideal for lowering investment risk.

Gaps in the Pre-Market

Pre-market trading refers to trading activities that occur between the hours of 8 a.m. and 9:30 a.m. EST on each trading day. This is usually done before the start of the regular market session. While waiting for the regular trading session, traders and investors monitor the pre-market trading period to judge the direction and strength of the market. There is limited liquidity and volume during pre-market activity. During the pre-market period, wide bid-ask spreads are common. Many retail brokers, despite offering pre-market trading, limit the types of orders that can be used during this period. Direct-access brokers begin to allow access to pre-market activity as early as 4 a.m. It is critical to remember that there is little activity during the pre-market period.

Gapper and dumper stocks are the most reliable types of stocks to trade during pre-market hours. They are usually viable during the seasons when various companies' earnings are reported. During this time of year, these stocks gap with the volume, either up or down. They are typically set off by a primary catalyst, such as press releases, news, or earnings reports. They could also be reacting to rumors, analyst upgrades or downgrades, or both. It is important to note that when stocks gap in response to earnings reports and guidance, they tend to get more 'tradability, follow through, and consistent volume. When trading during pre-market hours, keep in mind that there are fewer participants, a wider spread, and thin liquidity. It is not advisable to trade pre-market unless there is a significant volume gap caused by a catalyst. For most traders, waiting for the market to open is the best option.

CHAPTER 7:

WHY MOST DAY TRADERS LOSE

With so many advantages to day trading, it begs the question of why so many day traders fail. Why do the majority of these traders fail if the activity is as profitable as it sounds? Understanding why traders fail provides some insight into the common mistakes that traders make that cause them to lose money. As a result, you'll be in a better position to trade wisely by avoiding common pitfalls in such trading. Here are a few of the reasons why traders fail.

Relying on Chance

Assume there is a new trader in the market named John. John has some market knowledge because he is constantly watching the news, particularly the stock market. John, on the other hand, has never traded. He believes he can try day trading because he has some basic market knowledge. To this point, John has never sat down to write down some stock trading strategies that he could use. So, without thinking, he opens an account and buys 400 shares.

Fortunately for him, the stock market rises during his lunch hour. After lunch, John decides to liquidate his holdings. His first sale nets him a profit of $100. His second attempt earns him $100 as well.

Now, John has the impression that he is a competent trader. He has earned $200 in a single day.

After careful consideration of John's situation, an experienced trader would argue that John's day trading activity could be fleeting. In John's case, if he gains the impression that his strategies are working, he risks losing money. Interestingly, he may be tempted to increase his stake because he knows he will profit. It is critical to understand that John's strategies have not been tested. As a result, there is no guarantee that his trading activity will generate returns in the long run.

The danger that John faces here is that he believes in the untested strategies that he has devised. As a result, he may overlook recommended trading techniques that would have assisted him in avoiding common blunders. Finally, if he loses money, he will be disappointed, claiming that day trading is not profitable. This is the trap that the majority of newcomers fall into. Their initial success in online trading blinds them to the importance of continuous learning in this activity.

Strategy Abandonment

Assuming John learned from his mistakes and avoided them in future trades. He now relies on a strategy that has helped him find success in day trading for the past year or two. At this point, John believes he has discovered the best strategy for him.

However, another issue arises as a result. John realizes that his strategy has resulted in losses six times in a row. He's in a pickle, not knowing what to do because he can't keep losing money. So, what does John do? He decides to try a different approach. Regardless of the success, he had with his previous strategy, John now believes it is time to try something new. Ideally, he will be implementing a new and untested strategy. One thing to keep in mind here is that John is attempting an untested strategy. He is abandoning a strategy that has served him well for the past two years. The danger here is that John will end up back where he started. He may suffer losses as a result of abandoning his strategy.

You should learn here that randomness can lead to profits as well as losses for a trader. To avoid such randomness, it is recommended that a trader have a solid plan that they follow. This is a strategy that will govern how they trade. A good strategy should lay out its entry and exit strategies. In addition, the plan should specify the money management technique that will assist a trader in using their money wisely.

Lack of Knowledge

Lack of Knowledge One of the main reasons why most traders fail is a lack of market knowledge. They are in a bind because they failed to educate themselves about stock markets. You cannot consider yourself a trader simply because you buy and sell stocks. Most emphatically not! You must learn how to analyze the securities you intend to purchase. Your broker may not provide you with all of the information you require to become a successful trader. So, don't assume that reading magazines and newspapers will provide you with the market information you require. A wise trader understands the importance of following a profitable trading strategy. They understand why it is critical for them to effectively analyze stocks to determine whether or not they are purchasing profitable stocks. More importantly, a wise traders should be aware of the best strategies for effectively managing their finances. Don't believe the day trading myths that are circulating on the internet. Do your due diligence by researching and educating yourself on stock markets.

Mindset Misalignment

We are emotional beings who live in a human world. Being overly emotional, on the other hand, can be dangerous in an uncertain trading environment. You must work on your emotions to become a successful trader.

The topic of trading psychology, which will be discussed later, will educate you on the significance of developing the proper mindset in online trading. Managing your emotions will have a significant impact on whether you end the day with losses or profits. As a result, you must keep your emotions in check.

Adaptability to Market Changes

One thing you can count on is that trading markets will always fluctuate. There is no guarantee that a specific market will rise steadily throughout the buying and selling period. If this were true, everyone would have been a trader. The best traders will always be able to adapt to market changes. They will be able to tell when to buy and when to sell. Before investing in a specific stock, it is a good idea to run a scenario analysis. Following that, you should devise strategic moves to ensure that you make profits while minimizing the possibility of incurring losses.

Making Mistakes and Learning

People frequently say that failing is a necessary part of succeeding. This is correct. Unfortunately, it is one of the primary reasons that day traders fail. A day trader will lose a lot of money if they learn by making mistakes here and there. Most traders are put off by the prospect of putting their money in stocks because of the need for trial and error. Some people even argue that day trading is a form of gambling. To avoid this issue, one should learn from more experienced traders. You will reduce your chances of losing money this way. Similarly, you will learn how to use market volatility to your advantage. As a result, do not choose to learn how to trade by trial and error. You will only lose a lot more money than you anticipated.

Unrealistic Predictions

Take a break! Day trading is, in fact, a profitable activity that can earn you a living. Nonetheless, you should not be blinded by the fact that losses are possible. Day trading will not make you rich overnight. However, it is a slow and gradual process in which your money will multiply. Traders fail because they try to force returns to compensate for their massive losses. Having a solid plan and sticking to it will assist you in lowering your expectations. You should always keep in mind that you are trading for a living. As a result, patience is essential.

Inadequate Financial Management

The effort you put into developing a viable strategy is the same effort you should put into managing your finances. A trader should stick to a plan that specifies how much money they will risk regularly. The money put at risk should provide the trader with the satisfaction that it is worth the rewards they expect. Having enough funds set aside for trading should not give the impression that one must spend their money on stocks. The more capital you have, the more you should preserve.

The bottom line is that traders can deal with the possibility of failure by following a strategy. Sticking to a trading plan shows that you are disciplined enough to know how much money you are willing to risk. It also implies that you will use a successful buying and selling strategy. Most importantly, you will give yourself enough time to learn everything there is to know about day trading.

CHAPTER 8:

CHARACTERISTICS OF WINNING TRADERS

Anyone can become a day trader, but to survive in the highly competitive market in the long run, you must adapt yourself to the needs of this business. You must cultivate some characteristics that will set you apart from the crowd and allow you to thrive as a day trader. Let's take a look at some of the traits of successful traders:

They Accept Complete Responsibility

Good traders accept their losses without dwelling on or blaming others or conditions. They learn from their mistakes and continue in business. For successful traders, there is a system.

They strictly adhere to their trading system. Many established traders are willing to accept responsibility for their success, but few are willing to accept failure.

There is no mention of the market-maker or broker winning in some way, the market behaving strangely, the system, their risk management, or their mind-influencing their trade. During a loss, however, these stumbling blocks suddenly appear at the forefront of their minds. When things don't go your way, it's natural to blame someone other than yourself, the one who pushed the buttons. Having a gut-level responsibility does not separate winners from losers. They are the same. In this case, they all stemmed from a common denominator - you. Will you boost your ego when you succeed, or will you use what you've done well to do even better? Trading serves as a mirror to oneself, allowing one to see what needs improvement and work on it while also recognizing and increasing what works. And the height of your earnings and success is determined by your weakest trading skill. Fortunately, skill is a drill that can be easily shaped to build the pillars of your success.

They Have a Great Deal of Patience

The majority of positions are known to successful traders the moment they are opened. They must wait for their opportunity. They have the patience to deal with all of the trading uncertainty. Most traders devise a strategy to help them determine when and where to enter a trade. If executed correctly, that strategy should generate a profit. It may appear simple, but traders face a problem: when they see a fast-moving chat in real-time, their minds are tricked into believing that you enter a trade before the market structure is fully developed.

You are afraid of losing trade, so you enter early and usually lose.

Wait for the right setup and then execute your trade. You must also be willing to pass up opportunities; only take trades that will provide you with the proper setup and trigger your trade. Unless the market dictates otherwise, there should be no trades.

Hold a brainstorming session to determine what you could do better if you are following your plan but still getting into it too soon. If the price is higher and begins to fall, consider waiting for that to happen before investing. When the price begins to move sideways, look for small indications that it is about to rise again. If the trend continues, waiting for the price to rise before entering the trade can be beneficial. If the price wiggles around during the pullback, consider looking for higher highs and higher lows within the pullback.

These movements indicate that buying pressure will resume.

When the price appears to shift opposite right before moving in the direction you expect, you are waiting for the move to occur before acting. Do not trade until you are certain that this is the right time to do so. To make a profit, you do not need to capture every significant price movement. When you skip a step, you're missing it.

Be patient; the market moves more slowly than we would expect.

Waiting for the right setup and trigger will allow you to catch more of the price movements you anticipate and avoid losing money on losing trades.

They are foresighted.

Successful day traders cannot become enslaved by the past. Although day traders use historical data to make trading decisions, they must also be able to apply the information in real-time. Traders are also planning their next moves, deciding what to do based on where the market is headed.

The markets do not remain static. We cannot decide in five minutes that we are going to buy at a certain price and then forget about all of the market knowledge that has occurred during those five minutes. Day traders are constantly planning their next move based on new market information that they receive every second. They consider various scenarios that could occur and then plan how they would execute their trading strategy in each of those scenarios.

They do not engage in overtrading.

Overtrading is the unneeded purchase or sale of financial instruments. In many ways, having too many open positions on a single trade or using an excessive amount of capital. There are no laws or regulations prohibiting individual traders from overtrading, but it can harm your portfolio. Overtrading can have serious consequences for trading brokers, who are regulated entities. It is best to avoid overtrading and to have a well-thought-out trading strategy and risk management strategy in place. Stop trading emotionally: distinguish between logical and emotional trading decisions and provide sound reasoning for your decisions.

When you already have multiple open positions, spreading your investment across asset classes can help reduce risk.

Using only what you have: decide how much you want to gamble, but never trade with more money than you can afford to lose.

Overtrading should be avoided by good traders. They are aware that overtrading puts their account at risk, and not everyone is aware that it is the day of the trade. They are most likely anticipating an opponent.

They Can Be Modified

Successful traders can adapt. They personalize their trading strategies and market-moving decisions. Successful traders are aware of the type of dealer they are.

They do not force themselves to trade in methods or strategies because their personality is not compatible. After a full month of trading, you may make minor changes to your trading plan based on what you learned from your trading plan review sessions. Trades centered on these minor strategic improvements should be carried out for another month and then evaluated. Changes to the plan should not be made before the one-month mark because it is too easy to make changes based on individual trades rather than overall results. The issues raised in your self-review are being addressed daily. All you have to do for the self-review is stick to your trading strategy, whatever it may be. If the trading strategy evolves, so will your company, but it is always your responsibility to adhere to the strategy. Your daily self-examination does not affect the trading plan; rather, you are working on your personality traits to follow the plan. Weekly, strive to make minor changes to your trading strategy. The same idea applies to your daily self-evaluation. Work on only one thing at a time. Attempting to solve multiple problems at once implies that you are not focusing enough on each problem because your attention is being spread too thinly.

They Take Action

They Act Successful traders act on their ideas. They do not allow them to control their fear of their choices, and they do not interfere with their business. They make use of proven systems. Their commercialization and metrics are centered on high probability, sound trades, money management, keeping its strategy curve free of tying and incorporating their program into their business plans. It is not sufficient to simply watch videos or read. Before becoming sufficiently determined to make trade decisions in ever-changing market conditions, day traders must regularly practice what they are learning.

It's not just about putting in the hours. It is possible today to trade for years, putting in hundreds or thousands of hours and never seeing any progress because you are not focused on a specific activity. To practice effectively, concentrate on a single activity.

This is where the intention to exchange comes into play. A trading plan is a document that specifies how, why, and when a trader enters and exits trades, how they control risk, and the size of their position. It also specifies which markets and when they will be traded. Implementing a plan to track progress is part of the practice.

Day trade in a demo account, one component of the trading strategy at a time, until the strategy becomes second nature. You could, for example, go through charts and select entry points for your strategy. Do this until you've identified all of the entry points provided by your strategy. Day trading necessitates quick reflexes and precise timing.

Practice so that, depending on the technique, entries occur exactly when they should. Then proceed to adjust the stop-loss. Then practice correctly positioning the income target. Practice having the ideal position size on each trade and every other trading element covered by the trading plan. While it may appear strange, you are also learning what not to do the entire time.

Your goal is not only to follow through on your strategy and execute all of the trades you are told to execute (when the circumstances are favorable, based on your trading plan), but also to practice sitting on your hands when your strategy does not require you to do so. Trading is as much about the deals you don't do as it is about the ones you do. If your plan does not include a trade incentive, do not implement it. Most new traders lack the patience required to wait for a legitimate trade signal, but it is something that can be learned with practice.

When a legitimate trade opportunity presents itself, practice being cautious and pounce. Traders will devote different amounts of time to each component of their trading strategy. Each item of the trading plan will typically take 15 to 20 days to complete. After about six months of using this method, a trader should have a clear understanding of their trading plan, have practiced their strategy for days, and have a reasonable idea of how to use it under all market conditions.

They are well-disciplined.

Discipline is a key characteristic that every trader requires. The market provides you with virtually limitless trading opportunities. Every second of the day, thousands of different items are exchanged, but only a small percentage of those seconds provide excellent commercial opportunities.

If a strategy provides four to five trades per day, stop loss and goals are automatically set for each trade. During the day, there are only about five seconds of active trading.

CHAPTER 9:

WHAT IS BEST TO TRADE?

When it comes to stock purchases and sales, it is entirely up to the investor to select whatever he or she believes will be a good investment. It is difficult to generalize the type of stock that will suit everyone because there is no one-size-fits-all rule.

However, the following are the types of stocks that can be traded on the stock exchange.

Stocks of a Corporation

Company stocks are those that a company issues to its employees as well as the general public. Although top companies do not directly offer their shares to the public, employees who own them can sell them on the market. There are numerous multinational corporations to choose from,

59

such as Microsoft, Coca-Cola, Intel, Apple Inc., Nokia, and others. You can select a company that you believe will assist you in increasing the value of your investment. You will need to research which companies are doing well and which are not, and then decide which ones to invest in. But don't be in a rush to find the best stocks for you. Take your time and keep an eye on the trend for a few months. Once you've established a pattern, you can begin purchasing the company's stock.

Commodities

The commodities market is a place where various commodities are bought and sold. These commodities can be classified as follows:

Agricultural

Food items such as vegetables, fruits, pulses, and other crops are examples of agricultural commodities. Each commodity has a different price, and you can decide to invest in them based on which crops are doing well. These commodities are ideal for day trading because their value generally rises by the end of the day. Potatoes, pulses, rice, and sugar are among the most popular commodities.

Metal

Metals are a good market for investors as well. Metals with high market value include copper, nickel, iron, and lead. You can trade in these metals, but you must look for the ones that are currently performing well. You can choose to keep them for a set period and then sell them before the deal expires.

Industrial

Industrial solvents, chemicals, and other liquid commodities are also in high demand. They are always in high demand and command high prices. You can invest in the ones that you believe will sell for a good price.

Energy

Crude oil, petroleum, paraffin, and other energy resources are also traded. These are required to fuel your cars and are used in cosmetics, among other things.

As a result, they are always in high demand. You can select one that you believe is in high demand and trade with them.

Livestock

Livestock, like other commodities, is traded daily in the stock market. Pigs, sheep, and other animals fall into this category. Weather conditions, diseases, and market demand and supply are just a few of the factors that can influence their prices.

These are the various types of commodities from which to choose, and you can buy one type or diversify by buying several types.

Currencies

When it comes to day trading, the investor has the option of trading in currencies. As an investor, you have a lot of options and flexibility when it comes to hedging your currency risk. Currency options, or FX options as they are commonly known in the options markets, allow the same core hedging and trading strategies as options on ETFs, stocks, and indexes. The best and simplest way to remember what type of "option" you need to trade on is to concentrate on the base currency or the first currency in each currency pair. The quote currency, also known as the counter currency, is the second currency in the pair. Prices for "options" are typically derived from the base currency and are expressed relative to the quote currency. For each of the ten FX pairs, a USD-based currency pair (per USD) is available. For example, if you believe the US dollar will strengthen against the Japanese yen, you would buy YUK calls. When you anticipate that the yen will strengthen against the US dollar, you buy YUK puts. It is up to you to decide what you believe is best suited for trading based on the resources you have available.

You don't need extensive knowledge of these products, and even a basic understanding is sufficient to determine whether the products are worth investing in.

Index

Index trading is a type of trading in which you bet on the rise and fall of an index. Each sector of the stock exchange will have an index that takes into account the prices of all stocks listed in that sector. Then divide it by the number of stocks in the market to get a specific number. All of these indexes are now combined, and a final index, representing the collective index of the entire stock market, is created. You can now "bet" on where the index will end up at the end of the day. You must research individual indexes such as the IT industry index, the consumer goods index, and so on. You can invest in the index once you believe you know where it will be at the end of the day.

ETF

Exchange-Traded Funds (ETFs) are another name for ETFs. These ETFs function similarly to mini mutual funds that are traded on the market. Each ETF will be comprised of a variety of underlying securities, which will be divided into several small pieces. These can be purchased in bulk and traded daily.

The main idea is to purchase them at a low cost and then sell them at a higher cost. You must understand that they are slow movers, and you must buy them and wait for their value to increase.

These are much preferred because they provide the benefits of a mutual fund while being able to be traded daily.

Bonds

Bonds are securities issued by companies that can be bought and sold for a profit. These bonds can take several forms, which are described below:

Government Issued Bonds

The term "government bonds" refers to bonds issued by the government. As you may be aware, the government requires funds from time to time and will request that you pay them forward. When you do, they will issue you a bond with a much lower value than its actual value.

When it matures, you can collect the amount you paid as well as the interest that they would have paid you. If you want to sell the bond at any time, you can, and you will be paid a higher price for it. The government may also agree to pay you a certain percentage of interest each month, and you can take advantage of this opportunity to keep your money safe while also earning a profit.

This type of investment is extremely safe because the government will not fail to pay you when you are due money.

Bonds issued by agencies

Agency bonds are similar to government bonds. They are run by government-funded corporations. As a result, these can be classified as government bonds. They will pay you a high-interest rate on your investment. However, they do not provide the same level of security as government bonds. You may also be required to invest a set amount of money. However, given their success rate, they are an excellent choice for anyone looking to protect their money while also earning a certain rate of return on it. When it comes to liquidating agency bonds, the same rules apply. You can either sell them at a higher price or collect your principal and interest when they mature.

Federal Government Bonds

Federal bonds are issued by your local governments. Local governments will issue bonds in the same way that the federal government does. These bonds can be purchased at low-interest rates and held for a long period. You can sell them whenever you want and earn more money. These bonds will pay you more than government bonds because your local government will not require a large sum of money for a large-scale project that will be relatively low-key. This type of investment will be far superior to saving in a bank, which will pay you far less interest.

Bonds issued by corporations

Corporate bonds are those that are issued by businesses. Multinational corporations, as you are aware, require funding for their projects as well.

This money will be raised by selling bonds to the general public. They will agree to repay you after some time and will pay you a fixed rate of interest until then. These bonds can be sold for a profit at any time. However, you must understand that these companies will not provide you with a guarantee in the same way that your government and federal government bonds will. As a result, it will be a risk that you are willing to take.

However, if you choose a large multinational corporation, you may strike gold. You will not only be paid more, but you will also gain their loyalty. They might be willing to give you discounted shares in their company, which is a plus for you. You can then sell these stocks for a large profit at a later date!

Zero-Coupon Bonds Due to their ease of trading, zero-coupon bonds are extremely popular. They are extremely liquid, and they are always in high demand. Let's say a zero-coupon bond is worth $500. When you buy it, they will give you $100 and ask you to exchange it for $500 in two years. So, despite its current value of $100, you will receive four times that amount after exchanging it in two years. As a result, not only will your money be safe, but you will also be able to multiply its value several times over.

CHAPTER 10:

HOW MUCH DO YOU NEED TO DAY TRADE?

Before starting any business, one would like to know how much capital they will require. The same is true for day trading. The amount of capital required from them is an important question that most investors would like to know. The amount of money required to day trade will vary depending on the market in which you wish to invest. Your trading style will also have an impact on the amount of money you need to raise. Different markets will necessitate different amounts of capital. The following is a breakdown of the various markets available to you, as well as the capital requirements for each.

Capital Needed by Stock Traders

If you want to trade stocks, you should have at least $25,000 saved up for the transaction. You are not restricted to this sum of money. If you intend to trade more than three times, you should have more than $30,000. You will be unable to trade if your trading account falls below USD 25,000. You must top up your account to the required minimum balance. The account balance minimum here applies only to traders who want to invest in US stocks. It is important to understand that the minimum account balance required to invest in other stocks in global markets will vary. The country in which you rise may not have a minimum balance requirement. Regardless, it is advisable to deposit a reasonable amount that will allow you to profit from each buying and selling activity that you engage in. What is the point of saying this? In some cases, lower balances are simply eaten up by commissions and transaction costs. As a result, you will not notice any changes in your account as a result of these deductions.

Most market traders will always struggle with a lack of capital. Inadequate capital will prevent you from profiting from market volatility. You may have incurred losses now, but you may be able to recoup your losses later if the stock market unexpectedly rises. As a result, having enough capital is highly recommended.

Forex Traders' Capital Requirements

The forex market is not the same as the stock market. Smaller sums of capital are required in this case. This should be good news for a newbie like you. You can start day trading in forex today with the small amount of money you have saved up. The benefit of forex is that you can take advantage of the leverage provided, which can be up to 50:1.

In some countries, this figure could even be higher. An increase in leverage implies a higher risk that could be met with a spectacular reward.

Because of its liquidity, forex trading is an excellent choice for day trading. The forex market is the world's largest. Daily, the amount of money in circulation typically exceeds $5 trillion. As a result, the liquidity of this market makes it very appealing. So, how much money do you need to start trading forex? You can start trading with as little as $100. Nonetheless, the suggested amount is $500. This allows you to purchase currencies at optimal stop levels.

As you can see, this is a small sum of money that you will need to start this activity. You can't say you'll make a living off of it. It is important to remember, however, that you can gradually raise capital with your daily earnings. In line with this, just because you are new to forex trading does not mean you should overlook the importance of starting small.

Futures Capital Requirements

In addition to stocks and forex, you will have the option of investing in futures. The advantage of futures is that you can invest in them with a small amount of money. There is no legal minimum balance required to invest in futures contracts.

However, a trader must have sufficient capital to cover day trading margins within a given day. A lot of brokers will require a trader to have a $1,000 minimum balance. Brokers will require a $400 minimum balance if you are trading E-mini S&P 500 (ES) futures. This is the maximum day trading margin you can have. Regardless of whether you are limited to a specific balance, you should aim to start with a realistic balance of at least $8,000. Other futures will require additional margins from your broker for you to trade effectively. As a result, before signing up for anything, you should confirm with your trader.

Finally, in terms of the amount of money required, it is clear that different markets will necessitate different capital amounts. Trading stocks is not recommended if you are on a tight budget because it is capital intensive. Forex, on the other hand, allows you to begin trading with as little as $1,000. Nonetheless, it is advised that you have more to ensure that you have a buffer. When working with limited funds, futures are also a great option.

It should also be stated that trading with your capital is never a good idea at first. Use demo accounts to trade with virtual money when working with a broker. Once you've determined that your trading strategies work for you, you can begin using real money.

The advantage gained here is that you can easily identify potential mistakes when using your money. As a result, it saves you from putting your money at risk.

Establishing Your Risk Tolerance

Aside from knowing how much money you'll need to trade, you should also take some time to define your risk tolerance. What exactly do we mean by "risk tolerance"? It denotes the amount of unpredictability in investment returns that a trader is willing to accept. As a trader, you should have a thorough understanding of your ability to withstand large market swings. When markets appear to be falling, it is natural to panic. In such cases, you may end up selling at an inopportune time. As a result, you should be aware of your risk tolerance at this point. How much risk are you willing to take in day trading? You should evaluate your previous performance to clearly define your tolerance capacity. Determine the worst-case scenarios in which you have felt comfortable incurring losses.

Several factors can influence your risk tolerance capacity. For example, if you have a high chance of earning more money shortly, this will influence how much you can stomach. Also, if you want to take advantage of future securities, such as a pension, your risk tolerance will be high. In general, you will be prepared to face significant risks if you are confident that you have other assets that can generate additional income.

The various types of risk tolerance are described below.

Risk Tolerance Is Aggressive

Traders with extensive experience in day trading will find it simple to accept the risk of investing in highly volatile securities. This is because they are well-versed in market trends. They can easily predict the next trend of specific security due to their expertise. They frequently can tolerate market fluctuations. On a good day, they maximize returns while taking the highest risks. This is the essence of aggressive risk tolerance.

Tolerance for Moderate Risk

Moderate traders will take some risks but will avoid overly risky securities. In this case, they will seek out less volatile markets. Their primary goal is to reduce the risks that they are likely to face.

Conservative risk Tolerance

Conservative traders are not the same as aggressive or moderate traders. As the name implies, these investors will make every effort to minimize risks at all costs. The majority of traders in this category are retirees.

Where do you stand based on the information provided? How risk-averse are you? You should be aware that your tolerance capacity will evolve as you learn to cope with losses. However, you must understand what works best for you from the start.

The significance of this is that you will keep yourself from giving up every time you suffer unexpected losses. Knowing your risk tolerance is an important part of your trading foundation, and it will help you grow into a successful trader.

CHAPTER 11:

CHOOSING WHAT TO TRADE?

There are thousands of equities to choose from for a trader, and day traders have no restrictions on the types of stocks they can trade; you can trade on virtually any stock of your choice.

With so many options available, deciding which stock to add to your watch list may appear to be a difficult task. This brings us to the first step in day trading: deciding what to trade.

Here are some pointers to help you select the best stocks for maximum profit:

Day trading has a high level of volatility and liquidity.

In financial markets, liquidity refers to how quickly one can buy or sell an asset in the market. It can also refer to the effect of trading on the price of a security. It is easier today to trade liquid stocks than other stocks, and they are also more discounted, making them less expensive.

Liquid stocks have a higher volume in the sense that they can be purchased and sold in larger quantities without having a significant effect on the price. Because day trading strategies rely on precise timing and speed, high volume makes it easier for traders to enter and exit trades. Depth is also important because it indicates the level of liquidity of stocks at various price levels that are below or above the current market offer and bid. Furthermore, corporations with higher market capitalizations have more liquid equities than corporations with lower market capitalizations because it is easier to find sellers and buyers for stocks owned by these large corporations. Stocks with higher volatility also use day trading strategies. A stock is considered volatile if the corporation that owns it experiences more cash flow fluctuations. The financial market's uncertainty creates a large opportunity for day trading. During the day, online financial services such as Google Finance and Yahoo Finance regularly list highly volatile and liquid stocks. This information is also available on the websites of other online brokers.

Think About Your Situation

Because there is no one-size-fits-all solution in the financial market, the stocks you choose must be aligned with your goals and personal situation. You must consider your capital, risk tolerance, and the type of investment you intend to undertake. Let us not forget the importance of research in all of this. Your best bet is to educate yourself on the financials of various companies, research the market, consider the sectors that best reflect your values, personality, and personal needs, and start early. You must be familiar with market openings and be able to time yourself to follow these openings. When day trading, avoid becoming emotionally attached to a particular stock. Remember that you are looking at patterns to determine when it is best to exit or enter to minimize your losses and maximize your profit.

While you do not need to be glued to your screen, you do need to be aware of the earning season and the economic calendar.

This will assist you in selecting the best stocks for day trading.

The Internet of Things

This industry is also an appealing target for day traders, as several online media companies, such as Facebook and LinkedIn, have high trading volumes for their stocks. There have also been several debates about these social media companies' ability to convert their massive user bases into a sustainable revenue stream.

Although stock prices, in theory, represent the discounted cash flow of the companies that issued them, recent valuations also consider these companies' earning potential. According to some analysts, this has resulted in a higher stock valuation than the fundamentals would suggest. Regardless, social media is still a popular day trading stock.

Services about finance

Stocks in the financial services industry are also excellent for day trading.

Bank of America, for example, is one of the most actively traded stocks per trading session. Despite the increased skepticism that the banking system is facing, stocks from Bank of America should be among your top considerations if you are looking for company stock to day trade. Bank of America has a high trading volume, making it a liquid stock. Morgan Stanley, Citigroup, JP Morgan & Chase, and Wells Fargo are also affected. They are all characterized by volatile industrial conditions and high trading volumes.

Extending Your Geographical Boundaries

You must diversify your portfolio when trading in the financial market. Examine stocks listed on other exchanges, such as the London Stock Exchange (LSE) or the Hang Seng in Hong Kong. Extending your portfolio will give you access to potentially cheaper alternatives as well as foreign stocks.

Instability ranging from moderate to severe

To make money as a day trader, one must understand price movement. As a day trader, you can choose between stocks that move a lot in percentage terms and stocks that move a lot in dollar terms, as the two terms usually produce different results. Stocks that move 3% or more daily have consistently large intraday moves to trade. This also applies to stocks that trade above $1.50 daily.

Group Adherents

Although some traders specialize in contrarian plays, most traders prefer to invest in equities that move in lockstep with their index and sector group. This means that as the sector or index rises in value, so will the price of individual stocks. This is critical if the trader wishes to trade the weakest or strongest stocks daily. If a trader prefers to buy the same stock every day, it is best to concentrate on that stock and less on whether it corresponds with anything else.

Strategies for Entry and Exit

After you've chosen the best stocks in the world, your strategies will determine whether or not you profit from them. There are several day trading strategies available, but to increase your chances of success, you must follow certain guidelines and keep an eye out for specific intraday trading signals.

I'll go over five of these guidelines in more detail below:

Trade weak stocks when they are in a downtrend and strong stocks when they are in an uptrend.

To select the best stocks for day trading, most traders look for ETFs or equities that have a moderate to high correlation with the NASDAQ or S&P 500 indexes and then separate the strong stocks from the weak ones. This provides an opportunity for the day trader to profit because the strong stock has the potential to rise by 2% when the index rises by 1%. The greater the movement of a stock, the greater the opportunity for a day trader. As market futures/indices rise, traders should buy stocks that are rising more aggressively than the futures. With this, even if the futures market falls, it will have little or no impact on a strong stock. These are the stocks to trade in an uptrend because they offer more profit potential when the market rises.

When futures or indexes fall, it becomes profitable to short sell stocks that have fallen more than the market. ETFs and stocks that are weaker or stronger than the market may fluctuate daily, but certain sectors may be relatively weak or strong for weeks at a time. Always choose the stronger stock when looking for one to trade. The same rule applies to short trades. As a short seller, you should isolate weaker ETFs or stocks so that when prices fall, you have a better chance of profiting by being in the EFTs or stocks that fall the most.

Only trade with the current intraday trend.

The trading market always moves in waves, and as a trader, it is your job to ride these waves. When there is an uptrend, your focus should be on taking long positions, while when there is a downtrend, your focus should be on taking short positions.

We've already established that intraday trends don't last forever, but you can place one or more trades before the trend reverses. When the dominant trend shifts, you should start trading with the new trend. It may be difficult to isolate the trend, but Trend lines can provide simple and useful entry and stop-loss strategies.

Please take your time. Wait for the Retraction

Trend lines serve as visual guides, indicating where price waves will begin and end. As a result, when selecting stocks to day trade, you can use a trend line to gain an early entry into the next price wave. When you want to enter a long position, be patient and wait for the price to move down to the trend line and then back up before buying.

Before an upward trend line can appear, a lower price low must occur before a higher price low.

To connect the two points, a line is drawn that extends to the right. When short selling, the same principle applies. Wait for the price to move up to the downward-slope trend line, and then enter when the stock begins to move back down.

Take Profits regularly

As a day trader, you only have so much time to make money, so you should spend as little time as possible on trades that are losing money or moving in the wrong direction. Let me show you two simple guidelines for profiting when trading with trends:

Take your profits slightly below or at the former price low in the current trend if you are in a short position or downtrend.

Profits should be taken in a long position or uptrend at or slightly above the previous price high in the current trend.

When the market is stalling, do not play.

The market does not always follow a trend. Intraday trends can reverse so frequently that it is difficult to establish a dominant direction. If there are no major lows and highs, make sure the intraday movements are large enough to increase the chances of profit while lowering the risks of loss. For example, if you are risking $0.15 per share, the EFT or stock should move enough to give you a profit of at least $0.20 - $0.25 using the guidelines outlined above. When the price is not trending (moving in a range), switch to a range-bound trading strategy. During a range, the angled line will be replaced by a horizontal line. However, the general concept remains: buy only when the price falls to the lower horizontal area (support) and then begins to rise. Short sell when you notice the price has reached the upper horizontal line (resistance) and is starting to fall again.

Your buying strategy should be to exit close to, but not exactly at, the top of the range. Your shorting strategy should be to exit near the bottom of the range, but not exactly at the bottom. Place a stop loss just above the most recent high or just below the most recent low before entering a short signal or just below the most recent low before entering a buy signal.

Many traders find it difficult to alternate between range trading and trend trading, so they choose one or the other. If you choose range trading, you should avoid trading during trends and instead focus on trading ETFs or stocks that tend to range. If you want to trade trends, avoid trading when the markets are ranging and focus on trading ETFs or stocks that have the potential to trend.

CHAPTER 12:

HAVE THE RIGHT MINDSET

Day, Trading can be a difficult journey if you feel your mental energy has run out and you are unable to focus on the markets. Fortunately, you can overcome this issue and resume enjoying trading by changing your mindset. Some people believe that stock markets are inherently immoral, but the truth is that they are neither immoral nor moral. Stock markets lack emotion, so how you perceive the stock market to behave is entirely up to you. If you want to enter the stock market for the long term and also establish yourself as a full-time day trader, you must develop a specific mindset that allows you to observe the stock market objectively. Your mindset will determine how you react to various transactions.

It is your mindset that will determine how you react to lost trades and large profits. Your mindset will determine how you can remain calm in stressful situations and avoid emotional reactions. A trader who is disciplined and has a strong mindset will never allow emotions to influence his or her stock market decisions. Don't be concerned if this appears difficult to you; it should appear difficult to every beginner. Obtaining that status necessitates some effort. There is no way to become a successful trader overnight. Trading is a business, just like any other. You cannot become a disciplined trader overnight, just as you cannot become a successful businessman overnight. You must allow yourself enough time to achieve the success you desire.

The Importance of Having a Positive Attitude

The stock market is devoid of emotions, but market participants are usually overflowing with them. This is why reading chart patterns and trends work so well when trading. They demonstrate some well-known human patterns. That is how you, as a trader, can take advantage of market psychology.

A well-known proverb states that 90% of traders lose 90% of their money in 90 days. This is, to say the least, wicked, but it is still a popular phrase among traders. Before you invest in the stock market, you should consider what psychological characteristics the remaining 10% of traders possess. What characteristics distinguish them from the rest of the pack. If 90% fail, the money they lose will almost certainly go to the 10% who succeed. That's intriguing! Isn't that right? When you lose, your money is earned by someone else.

The people who earn your money are human beings just like you.

They are a small group of traders who have discovered the trading secret, which is nothing more than a trader's mindset. Trading psychology refers to a specific state of mind that a trader usually has while trading. The odds are stacked against you if you don't have the right mindset.

Day to Sharpen Your Trader's Mindset Traders can reshape their mindset by behaving calmly and relaxedly. You should not be concerned about your trades if you have adequate knowledge of the subject and have implemented proper risk management guidelines. If a trade hits the stop-loss level, it does not mean the end of the world for you. Traders consistently lose trades. Even professional traders with years of experience have experienced this. Professional traders who make their living by trading stocks have a winning percentage of 50%. Even at this rate, if you trade with the right mindset, you can make a good profit on your capital. You should develop the habit of not taking a losing trade personally. There is nothing personal about lost trade, though the temptation to make it personal is strong. Your mind may begin to race with the realization that you have lost something that you could have easily won or avoided. If you think like that, the need of the hour is to train your brain to believe that markets go up and down almost all of the time. As a day trader, you should remain confident in the market analysis that you have already completed. Simply follow the plan until the end of the day. Markets are devoid of emotions, and if you begin to succumb to your emotions, you will be unable to compete with traders who do not allow their emotions to interfere with their trading transactions throughout the day.

Create a morning routine to allow for a more relaxed trading session.

Try to get up earlier, do some exercise or yoga, and then sit at your desk with a heart full of faith in the homework you've completed for the day.

Learn, learn, and learn again!

The key to success in the stock market is education. It is one of the most important factors that contribute to the removal of fear from your brain. This is what distinguishes a good trader from a great trader. Even if you have nurtured and developed the proper trading mindset, you will not be able to succeed unless you have a solid knowledge base for the purpose. You must have a thorough understanding of the factors that influence price movements and market reactions. Similarly, I've hinted at how a market reacts to specific news and bonus reports regularly. This will strengthen your trader mindset.

Numerous concepts are worthwhile to learn. They cannot, however, be learned in a single session. Make it a habit to internalize a concept daily so that your brain has enough time to understand the subtle nuances of the concept and to apply it during trading without having to open a book. You can also make and keep notes in a small diary for future reference. You can establish a healthy routine by reading a good trading book an hour before going to bed to clear out your basic concepts and put them into practice during trading. You can also take trading classes to learn more about the stock market.

A Successful Day Trader's Mindset

Your psychology will be a major determining factor in achieving the trading results that you desire. Each trader has a distinct belief system, and it is their beliefs that govern how they trade and the outcomes they achieve. Even if they have the most profitable and seasoned trading strategy, traders with a weak belief system are more likely to fail. What exactly is a belief system? In layman's terms, it's known as 'The Trader's Mindset.' When dealing with psychological issues, it is in your best interest to track the issues in your brain, recognize them, and then find a solution to them. Otherwise, you will be unable to repair them. A psychologist recognizes the problems and then attempts to help the patient. Curing a problem can take longer because patients take their time recognizing the problem and accepting it as the source of their problems. If you want to heal as a day trader, you must accept responsibility for your problems.

Trading success is directly proportional to a well-functioning tracking system in your brain. It is also directly related to a successful money management strategy, sound psychology, and proper day capitalization. If you want to be successful in your trading endeavors, these must be in sync. Mastering your psychology is an ongoing process that will continue until you have complete control over your thoughts and decisions.

Psychological Problems

The most common psychological issue that day traders face is the fear of being stopped out or of posting a loss and exiting a position. It's a near-nightmare for day traders, and it makes them nervous. The fundamental reason for this behavior is that a trader is afraid of failure and believes that he will be unable to bear the loss. His ego is on the line. If you exit a trade too soon, you will lose profit, if not capital. It is quite common for a trader to exit a position to alleviate the anxiety and stress that an open position usually brings. In this sense, the greatest fear is the fear of reversal. Traders succumb to it once it reaches unprecedented proportions. They require gratification as well as assurance that their capital is now secure.

The most common mistake that day traders make is adding to a losing position. They're just doubling down on it. This type of behavior reflects a mindset that refuses to accept that it has lost the game. Again, the ego will not allow you to close your position and save your capital. Your brain pushes you to win from the same position in which you lost. If you have disclosed your positions to coworkers and family members, the problem becomes more serious. You are afraid of becoming a laughingstock in front of everyone.

Some traders refuse to accept responsibility for their trades. They can't accept that the market moved in the opposite direction that they expected it to. This type of mindset clouds their thinking, and they attempt to create a reality that corresponds to their expectations. Traders can sometimes enter the mindset of a gambler. They succumb to the euphoria of a bull market and drown in it by engaging in gambling. The gambler's mindset always tells you to ignore market indicators and to engage in compulsive trading even when the odds are stacked against you. Trading becomes an addiction for you. You continue to lose until your capital is depleted. This is extremely dangerous, and it must be checked.

Some people become enraged after losing a trading position.

Their brain informs them that they are victims of the market. Unrealistic expectations lead to frustration and anger among traders when they are shattered. This condition can occur if you become overly involved in a trade. You cannot control the market and turn it to your advantage simply by thinking in that manner. You may have expected the stock to rise during the day, but markets can take an unexpected turn at any time, leaving you stunned.

Too many expectations can lead to resentment, which can negatively impact your future trading transactions. This is not good for your profession. Excessive joy after winning a trading position is just as bad for your brain's health as excessive anger. This indicates a mindset in which you believe you have unrealistic control over the trade markets.

CHAPTER 13:

HOW TO OPEN AN ACCOUNT

Once you've mastered the fundamentals and are primed and pumped to invest in the stock market, you'll need a brokerage account to do so. You won't be able to buy stocks or invest in other securities unless you have this account.

This system has been modernized, and with the advent of computers and the internet, you can now make real-time trades through your brokerage firms. You will need to open a brokerage account for this.

A brokerage account is a contract between you and the brokerage firms to execute trades. The brokerage firm would provide you with software that would allow you to see the stock prices in real-time and bid on them at the price you desire. Simply deposit funds into your brokerage

83

account, and you will be able to purchase the securities you desire with this money.

Although the securities are purchased through the brokerage firm, you will be the sole owner of the assets, and the brokerage firm will only charge a brokerage fee on trades executed through it.

The process of opening a brokerage account is simple, but there are a few things to keep in mind. Cost, quality, and service are some of the factors that will be important to you in the end. You should also pay close attention to the brokerage fee charged by the firm, as this can be significant for a small investor. You must also consider the type of securities you wish to trade in.

Select the Type of Brokerage Account You Require

As a beginner, it is common for people to be perplexed by the variety of options available to them. The same thing can happen when deciding on the type of account you require.

For beginners, Robo Advisory services are the best option because they are less expensive and can assist you in long-term planning based on your investment and waiting potential. Robo advisor services charge low fees and have good algorithms to balance your funds based on your needs. Robo advisors are algorithm-based financial planning services that provide you with an automated, digital platform. Robo advisors will ask you detailed questions about your financial goals as well as the types of investments you can make, and based on that analysis, they will recommend investments that will work for you. The best thing about Robo advisors is that they will do the majority of the work and planning for you, so you won't have to keep up with the market as much. They will also perform rebalancing regularly to ensure that the funds remain in good condition.

They are very cheap, and you can open accounts with very small balances. Betterment, Wealthfront, Personal Capital, Bloom, and other popular Robo advisor accounts

Alternatively, if you want to get involved in the stock market and invest your time in it, you can open regular brokerage accounts and trade in a variety of asset classes such as stocks, ETFs, or Mutual funds. If you want, you can also choose to trade regularly. You will also need to consider taxes, which brings us to the question of whether you want to open a regular taxable account or an individual retirement account, as tax slabs differ in both. You should also consider whether you want to own and operate that account solely, or whether you want others in your family to have a role in it as well. Some brokerage firms that offer such accounts to beginners include Charles Schwab, Fidelity Investments, and Merril Edge.

The Price and Benefits

Brokerage firms charge fees and commissions, and numerous other costs vary by broker. Beginners should look for brokers with low fees and a greater emphasis on educating the trader. For a beginner, a simple platform with better access to knowledge is always preferable. Remember that you will be investing your hard-earned money, and you may not have much of it. When you arrive at the portal, you may feel overwhelmed. At that point, an interface that is both educational and simple is always beneficial. As a beginner, you should also look for brokers with low commissions.

Establishing a Brokerage Account

It is not difficult to open a brokerage account these days. Because most things are done online, there is very little paperwork involved.

However, this does not mean that the process of opening a brokerage account will be simple.

To open your account, you'll need to provide a lot of information.

Personal information such as your name, address, date of birth, and social security number will be required, as well a variety of other details such as your IRS Tax ID, signature, annual income, net worth, and employment status. You should not be afraid to share this information because it is necessary. You must understand that opening a brokerage account is a detailed process because you may have both short and long-term holdings in this account, and such information will be required. Aside from these questions, you may be asked about your investment objectives, financial goals, investment frequency, and risk tolerance. This is done to perform risk profiling, which aids in the evaluation of your financial goals. Better advisory services can be provided as a result of this. You may also be required to submit an acknowledgment of ownership of the account as well as an agreement that you will provide the information the broker-dealer requires.

You can then link your bank account to your brokerage account to easily transfer funds, and your account will be ready to use.

CONSIDER THE FOLLOWING POINTS

Fees and commissions

When you buy any stock, you will incur several fees and commissions. The price you bid on is not the actual price of the stock.

You will also have to pay brokerage fees, taxes, and settlement charges, which should be factored into your total cost calculation.

Brokerage firms will also charge you for a variety of other services.

Too

A brokerage account comes with a slew of fees. For example, you could be charged for inactivity fees, annual fees, research and data fees, trading platform fees, and a variety of other fees. You must be aware of the types of charges you may be required to pay at the end of the day to avoid unpleasant surprises in the form of unexpected expenses.

Consider the Frequency of Your Trades.

This is also an important point to remember. People who want to trade frequently want to keep their commissions as low as possible. Even a slightly higher commission can raise the cost of the trade for them. If, on the other hand, you do not intend to trade frequently and would only invest on occasion, it may be a good idea to look into the types of charges levied by the broker in the form of inactivity fees.

A good support system is beneficial.

As a beginner, prefer brokerages with a good support system because you may have frequent questions. If the brokerage firm lacks a good support system, you will have to rely primarily on the internet, and the advice you receive there may not be very accurate or precise.

CHAPTER 14:

TOOLS AND PLATFORMS

There are several tools that you will require to successfully carry out day trading. Some of these tools are available for free, while others must be purchased. Modern trading is not the same as traditional trading. This means that you must go online to access day trading opportunities. As a result, the most important tool you'll need is a laptop or computer with an internet connection. The computer you use must have enough memory to process your requests quickly. If your computer is constantly crashing or stalling, you will miss out on some lucrative opportunities. There are trading platforms that require a lot of memory to function properly, and you should always keep this in mind. Your internet connection must also be sufficiently fast. This guarantees that your trading platform loads in real-time. To avoid data lag, make sure you have an internet connection that can process data instantly. Because most internet providers experience outages, you may need to invest in a backup internet device, such as a smartphone hotspot or modem. You will also require the following tools and services:

Brokerage

To be successful in day trading, you must use the services of a brokerage firm. The firm's job is to carry out your trades. Some brokers have more day trading experience than others. You must choose the best day trading broker to help you maximize your profits from your transactions.

Because day trading entails multiple trades per day, you'll need a broker who charges lower commissions. You should also look for one that offers the best software for your transactions. If you prefer to use specific trading software for your transactions, look for a broker who allows you to do so.

Market Data in Real-Time

When it comes to day trading, market news and data are critical.

They provide you with the most recent market price changes, both current and anticipated. This data allows you to tailor your strategies accordingly. Professional day traders always spend a lot of money looking for this type of information on news platforms, online forums, or any other reliable channels. The price movements of specific stocks and commodities are frequently used to generate financial data. This information is available to the majority of brokers.

You will, however, need to specify the type of data you require for your trades. The type of data to obtain is determined by the stocks you wish to trade.

Monitors

Most computers have the capability of connecting to multiple monitors. Because of the nature of the day trading business, you must simultaneously track market trends, study indicators, follow financial news items, and monitor price performance. This is only possible if you have more than one processor, which allows the above tasks to run concurrently.

Classes

Although you can engage in day trading without attending school, you will need to be trained in some of the strategies required to succeed in the business. For example, you may decide to enroll in an online course to gain the necessary business knowledge. You may have all of the necessary tools, but if you lack the necessary experience, your efforts may be futile.

CHAPTER 15:

CHARTING

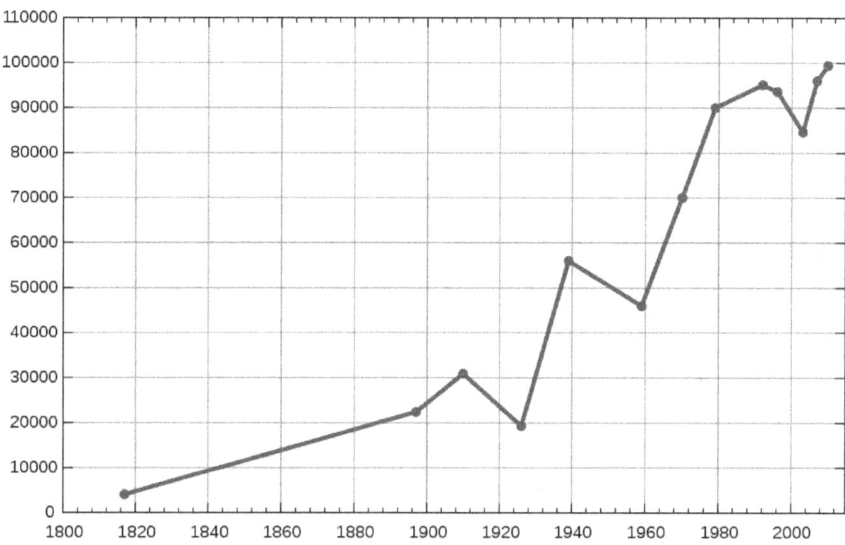

A chart is a graphical representation of the price of an asset over time. It has characteristics such as price point, price scale, and time scale. The price scale can be found on the right side of the chart by the day trader. From top to bottom, the scale goes from lowest to highest. Even though it is such a simple concept, the price scale can have a complex structure.

The space between the price points in a linear price structure is of equal size. If the difference between the first and second price points is 10, the difference between all price points will be the same. A logarithmic price structure has distances between two price points that change by an equal percentage. This means that if the price changes by 25%, it will apply to all price points.

The time scale, which is located at the bottom of the chart, is a date or time range. If he chooses a shorter timeframe, the day trader will see a more detailed chart with each data point displaying the asset's closing price. Some charts also display the open, high, low, and close prices.

An intraday chart can show price movements over a specific period in a single trading session. A day trader can expect a time scale of as little as five minutes. A daily chart can show a series of price movements, with each trading session represented by a single point, which can be the open, high, low, or close price.

CHART VARIETIES

Candlestick Diagram

This is a charting method that originated in Japan. To demonstrate a relationship, the method fills the interval between opening and closing prices. The closing points of these candles are indicated by color-coding. At any time, you will see black, red, white, blue, or green candles to represent the closing point.

Chart of Open-High-Low-Close (OHLC)

These are also known as bar charts, and they show the relationship between the highest and lowest prices in a trading period. They usually have a tick to show the open price on the left side and a tick to show the closing price on the right.

Graph with Lines

This is a chart that uses a line segment to map the closing price values.

Diagram with Points and Figures

This makes use of numerical filters that refer to times without fully utilizing the time to construct the chart.

Overlays

These are typically used on the main price charts and come in a variety of forms:

- Resistance – a price level that acts as the highest level above the normal price.
- Support is the inverse of resistance and appears as the lowest price value.
- A trend line is a line that connects two peaks or troughs.
- Two trend lines that are parallel to each other are referred to as a channel.
- Moving average – a type of dynamic trend line that considers the market's average price.
- Bollinger bands are charts that display the rate of volatility in a market.
- The average of the high, low, and closing price averages for a particular stock or currency is referred to as the pivot point.
- Indicators Based on Prices
- These examine the market's price values. These are some examples:
- Advance decline line – this is a market breadth indicator.
- The average directional index – indicates the market's strength of a trend.
- Commodity channel index – aids in identifying market cyclical trends.
- The relative strength index (RSI) is a chart that shows the price's strength.
- Moving average convergence (MACD) – the point at which two trend lines converge or diverge.
- Stochastic oscillator – this displays the close position that occurred within the most recent trading range.
- Momentum – This is a chart that shows how quickly the price changes.

Charts for Free

An intraday trader can use free charts that are available online, which provide the trader with not only technical analysis tools, but also advice, demonstrations, and guidelines on chart analysis.

Different free charts offer different features such as delayed futures data, real-time data, time frame selection, and indicator accessibility. Additionally, these charts allow a trader to participate in a variety of markets such as forex, futures, stock exchanges, and equity markets. Free Stock Charts and the Technician are two examples of free charts that an intraday trader can access and use for free.

Heiken-Ashi

Candles are used as the potting medium in Heiken-Ashi outlines, but the cost is defined numerically differently. Instead of the standard technique of candles deciphered from fundamental open-high-low-close criteria, costs are smoothed to all the more likely to show inclining value activity, as indicated by this equation:

Close = (Open + High + Low + Close)/2 Open = (Open + High + Low + Close)/4 High = Highest of High, Open, or Close

Lowest of the Low, Open, or Close

Usual terms

Average genuine range – The range over a specific period, typically day today.

Breakout – When a price breaks through a zone of support or resistance regularly due to an impending flood of purchasing or selling volume.

Cycle – Periods in which value activity must follow a specific example.

Dead feline skip – When prices fall in a down market, there may be an increase in cost as buyers come in accepting a small advantage or selling exaggeratedly. However, when vendors further depress the market, the transitory purchasing spell is known as a dead feline skip.

Average is the Dow hypothesis. Advocates of the hypothesis claim that if one of them begins to drift in a certain direction, the other will most likely follow. Many traders are interested in the transportation sector because it can provide insight into the economy's strength. A high volume of product shipments and exchanges indicates that the economy is in good shape.

Doji – A flame type characterized by a close to zero difference between the open and close value, indicating market trepidation.

Elliott wave hypothesis – The Elliott wave hypothesis proposes that markets go through repeating periods of good faith and cynicism that can be predicted and thus prepared for trading opportunities.

Fibonacci proportions – Numbers used as a guide to determine support and opposition.

Sounds – Harmonic trading is based on the possibility that value patterns repeat themselves, and market-defining moments can be identified using Fibonacci arrangements.

Fibonacci Sequences

Starting with 1 and adding the previous number, the Fibonacci number sequence develops. For example, 0 + 1 equals 1, 1 + 1 equals 2, 2 + 1 equals 3, 3 + 2 equals 5, 5 + 3 equals 8, and 8 + 5 equals 13. Fibonacci numbers are therefore 1, 2, 3, 5, 8, 13, 21, 34, 55, 89, 144, 233, and so on.

A Fibonacci number is equal to 1.618 times the Fibonacci number before it. A Fibonacci number, in turn, equals 0.618 times the Fibonacci number after it.

Analysts forecast changes in trends by employing four popular Fibonacci studies: arcs, fans, time zones, and, most notably, retracements. The retracement levels on a Fibonacci scale of 0–100 percent are 38.5 percent, 50 percent, and 61.8 percent. It's amazing how many creatures in nature, including humans, are proportioned precisely to those ratios.

Those familiar with Elliott Wave Theory are aware that wave counts follow the Fibonacci numbering sequence. As part of their charting features, many trading software platforms include Fibonacci studies. I will later recommend that you apply the retracements to your E-mini S&P futures chart.

"How fascinating," you mutter as you scratch your brow. "But what does this have to do with me making a lot of money in the market?"

Plenty. Particularly with the numbers 2, 3, and 5. We'll keep the numbers 2, 3, and 5 at the forefront of our minds from now on. These numbers appear frequently on charts, and we use them to forecast price movement. In later chapters, we'll go over Fibonacci levels in greater detail.

Stocks in strong uptrends typically move up for three days, then down (pull back) for two days. Alternatively, they move up for five days and then retrace for three days. In a downward trend, reverse those figures. Three days down, followed by two rally days, or five days down, three days up, is a likely pattern.

If a stock falls for four days in a row, you can bet it will remain in the red on the fifth. (This is always the case, except when it isn't.)

CHAPTER 16:

SUPPORT AND RESISTANCE

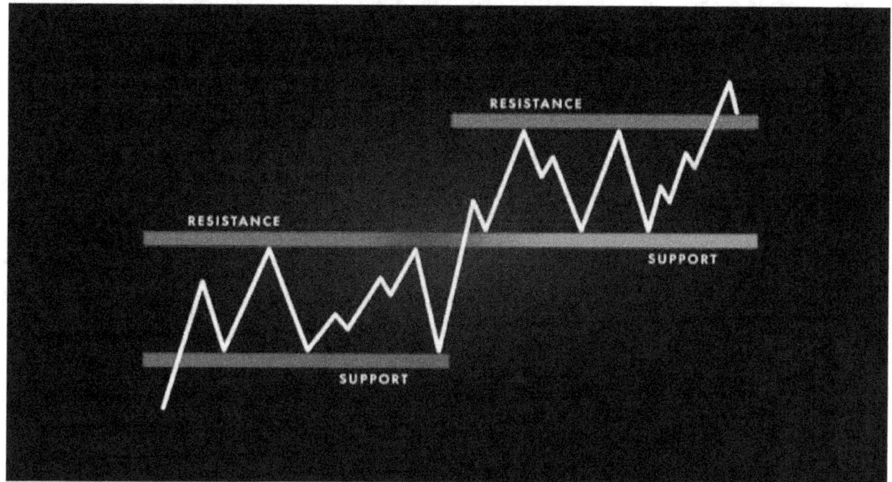

During an uptrend, resistance levels are price levels at which selling pressure tends to outnumber buying pressure, which can either interrupt or completely reverse an existing bullish trend. Resistance levels are typically represented by a horizontal line connecting consecutive high prices, also known as peaks or tops.

Support levels are price levels where buying pressure overwhelms selling pressure to the point where an ongoing downward trend is disrupted or reversed. A horizontal line is drawn beneath consecutive low prices, also known as bottoms or troughs, to represent support levels. Significant levels of support and resistance cause trend reversals, whereas minor levels of support and resistance only interrupt ongoing trends.

HERE'S HOW TO USE RESISTANCE AND SUPPORT LEVELS IN DAY TRADING:

Determine your SIPs or stocks/security holdings.

Check out the daily price charts of these SIPs before the markets open and look for significant or critical resistance and support price levels for your SIPs. Always keep in mind that support and resistance lines aren't always obvious, and there may be times when you can't find any. In such cases, do not impose anything that is not present. Simply employ other day trading strategies or examine your other SIPs to see if they have discernible resistance and support lines.

When the market opens, use a 5-minute chart to track the price movements of your SIPs. Look for indecision or Doji candlesticks as signals to enter long or short positions.

Buy long positions as close to the support lines as possible. Short positions should be sold as close to the resistance lines as possible.

When prices reach the next resistance or support level, you can begin closing or covering your long or short positions, respectively.

Close or cover half or more of your open positions at the following levels for optimal position management.

Then, in the next resistance or support level, close or cover the rest.

Set your stop-loss triggers at the support line for long positions, i.e., close your position and limit your losses if the price falls below the line. To minimize trading losses, cover short positions as soon as the price begins to rise above the resistance line.

If you're not sure how to draw support and resistance lines, here are some pointers to get you started:

The presence of indecision candles can help you identify areas of support or resistance. This is because these candles indicate areas where buyers and sellers compete on an almost even keel.

In many cases, whole and half-dollar prices serve as resistance or support levels, particularly for stocks priced less than $10 per share. Even if you don't see any support or resistance lines on these price points, keep in mind that these numbers could serve as very subtle, if not invisible, support or resistance lines.

The most recent points are the best for drawing these lines.

Price ranges

The more often support or resistance lines intersect extreme price points, the more accurate or reliable those lines are. Such lines should be prioritized.

The only relevant resistance and support lines are those that exist within the current price levels of the stock or security. It's pointless, for example, to look for such lines when a $7.50 stock was still trading at $13.80 or $2.45. Given that you're day trading and not taking medium to long-term positions, the chances of your SIPs' prices reaching those levels are practically nil.

Resistance and support lines are more like estimates or areas than precise price points. Prices may begin to bounce back within a few cents below or above $8.50 if the support line runs through this price level.

Solid resistance and support lines are those from which stock or security prices have rebounded. If prices do not bounce back from such lines, the chances are that it is not a legitimate resistance or support line.

You'd be better off drawing these lines across extreme daily prices or wicks, rather than across places in daily charts where a significant number of price bars have stopped. Why?

It's because past extreme low and high prices, i.e., tails and wicks, are primarily influenced by day traders, whereas price bars, i.e., candlestick bodies, represent daily open and closing prices, which are primarily influenced by longer-term traders or investors.

CHAPTER 17:

CLASSIC CHART PATTERNS

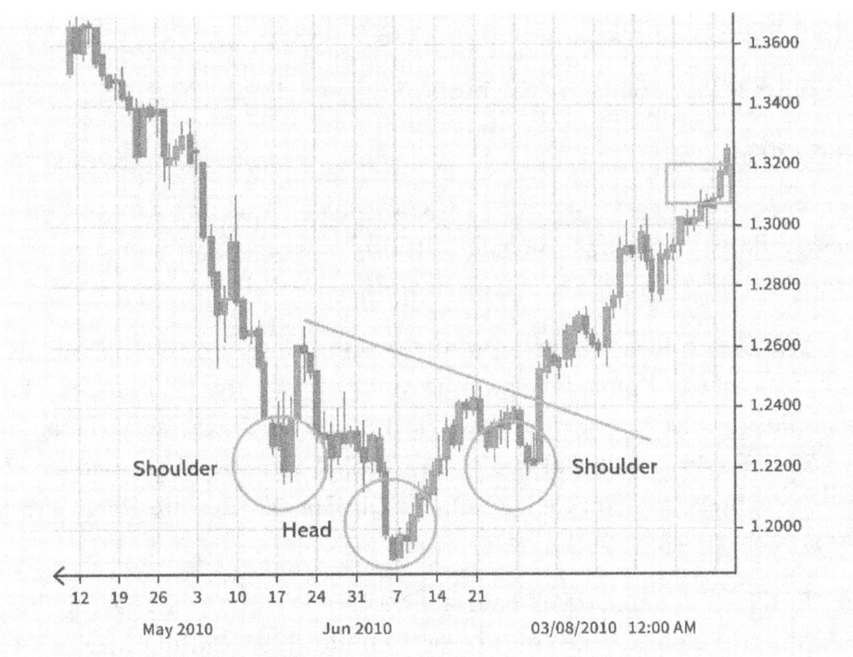

Chart patterns inform traders that the price is likely to move in one of two directions after the pattern ends. You must be aware of several patterns, including reversal and continuation. A reversal pattern indicates that the preceding movement will be reversed when the pattern is completed. A continuation pattern, on the other hand, indicates that the preceding pattern will be kept when the pattern is finished. Before you look at specific chart patterns, you should first understand a few concepts.

The most important is the trend line, which is drawn to show the commodity's level of support or resistance. A support trend line is a level below which the process finds it difficult to move. A resistance trend line depicts the level that a price finds difficult to breakthrough. Chartists employ a variety of patterns, which are listed below:

Shoulders and Head

This is a popular and reliable pattern for most traders who use technical analysis. The pattern, as the name suggests, resembles a head with shoulders. This is a reversal pattern that indicates that the price may move against a previous trend. When the pattern is completed, the price will almost certainly fall.

The pattern usually appears at the apex of an upward trend.

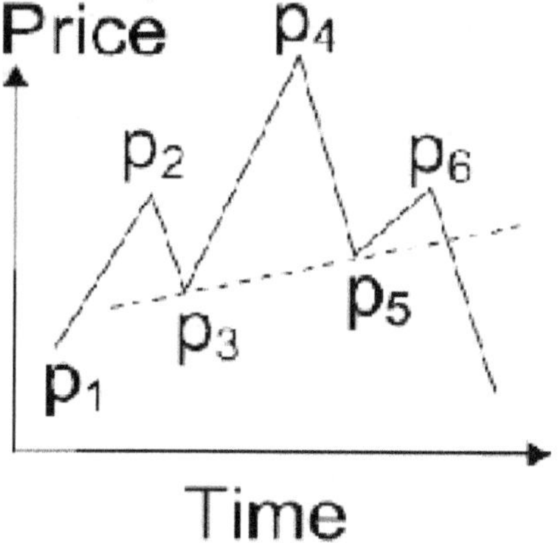

Another variation of the pattern is an inverted head and shoulder facing down. It usually appears during an upward trend and indicates that the price may rise.

Shoulders and Head Top

This indicates to the chart user that the price of a security is likely to fall. It is a trend reversal pattern that usually forms at the peak of an upward trend.

The pattern consists of four main stems that must be completed to show a reversal:

The formation of the left shoulder occurs when the commodity reaches a new high and then falls to a new low.

The formation of the head – once the price has reached its peak, it retracts to the formation of the other shoulder.

The formation of the right shoulder occurs when a peak lower than the peak in the head occurs.

When the price falls below the neckline, the pattern is complete.

Bottom of the head and shoulders

This pattern is exactly the opposite of the previous one. This signal indicates that the scrutiny will soon increase. The pattern usually appears when a downtrend ends and is considered a reversal pattern, with the direction going up after the pattern is completed.

Among the steps are:

Configuration of the left shoulder occurs when the price falls to a new low and then rises to a new high.

Head formation – when the price falls below the previous low and then rises to the previous high.

Right shoulder – this sells off, ending at a low price but higher than the previous one with a drop to the neckline.

The neckline is formed by the return to the previous level.

When the price rises above the neckline, the pattern is complete.

Handle and Cup

On the chart, this appears to be a cup. The pattern depicts a bullish persistence pattern in which the rising trend pauses and then trades downward before continuing in an upward trend at the pattern's conclusion. It can last from several months to a year, but the common form remains constant.

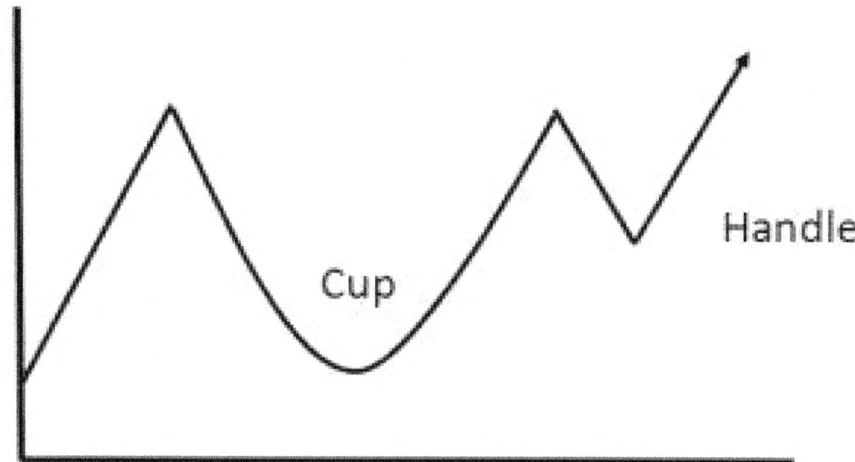

This is usually preceded by an upward move, which then comes to a halt and sells off. This is the beginning of the pattern, after which the security trades flat for an extended period with no discernible trend. The final component of this pattern, known as the handle, is a downward move that resumes the previous trend.

There are several components to the cup and handle that you should be aware of. To begin, you must understand that an upward trend occurs before the trend forms. The longer the previous trend, the less likely a large breakout is after the pattern is completed.

The Components

The cup's construction is critical; it should be nicely rounded, more of a semi-circle. The cup and handle pattern indicates that weaker investors are exiting the market while buyers remain for the commodity. If the shape is too sharp, it indicates that the signal is weakening.

You must also pay attention to the handle because it indicates the pattern's completion. The handle represents the commodity's descending move following the increasing move on the right side. A

103

downward trend line can be drawn during the move to form a breakout. A move above the trend line indicates that a previous upward trend is about to begin.

As with most patterns, volume must be considered to confirm the pattern.

A double top and a double bottom

These are signs of a reversal. They indicate a desire for security to maintain an existing trend. When this happens, especially when there are numerous attempts to run higher, the inclination reverses and a new trend begins.

Top of the World

This happens at the peak of an upward trend and indicates that the previous trend is failing and buyers aren't interested in the trend.

When the pattern is completed, the movement shows a reversal, and the commodity is expected to fall.

double top

The final stage of the pattern is the formation of new highs in the rising trend, after which the price begins to move towards the resistance stage. The pattern is complete when the price falls below the previous move's support level, signaling the start of a downward trend.

When using this pattern, you must wait until the price breaks below the key level before entering a trade. Doing so before the signal forms can have disastrous consequences because the pattern is only preparing for a reversal. The pattern depicts a push and pulls between sellers and buyers. Buyers are attempting to force the commodity through but are encountering opposition, preventing the rising trend from continuing. After a while, buyers decide to give up, and sellers seize control of the commodity, pushing it down on a new downtrend.

As previously stated, you must consider volume before deciding because you must consider the volume of the commodity when the price falls below a certain level.

Bottoms on both sides

The double bottom indicates an uptrend reversal. When the existing downtrend reaches a new low, the pattern forms. The move finds all support, preventing the commodity from falling further. When the movie finds the right support, the commodity will reach a new high, creating the commodity's resistance point. The following stage reduces the commodity to its lowest point.

However, the commodity finds some support and then reverses course.

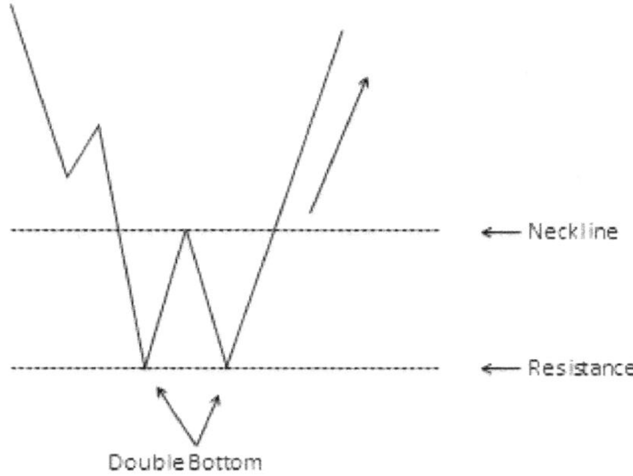

When the price rises above the resistance level encountered before the move, the pattern is confirmed.

For a definite reversal, the commodity must gain support to show a reversal in a downward trend.

Triangles

The names, as you can see from the previous chart patterns, leave little to the imagination. Triangle patterns, as the name implies, form a triangular shape.

The pattern's essential design is when two trend lines intersect, with the commodity's price moving between the two trend lines.

Triangles are classified into three types: symmetrical triangles, ascending triangles, and descending triangles.

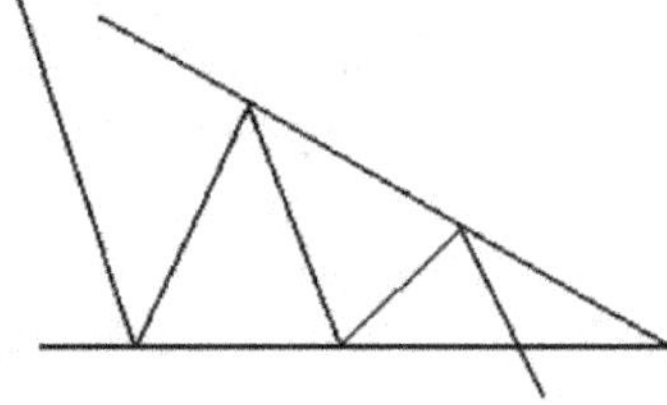

Ascending Triangle

Descending Triangle

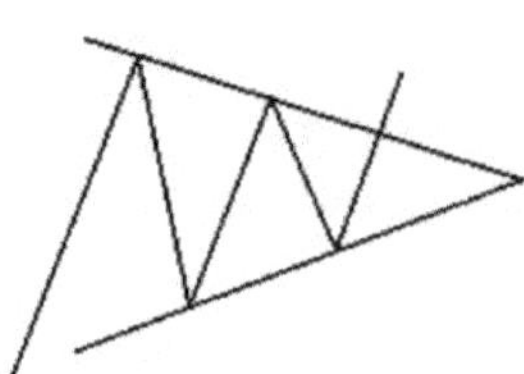

Symmetrical Triangle

Symmetrical Triangle

This is a continuation pattern that indicates a consolidation trend followed by the continuation of a previous trend.

A downward resistance line and an equally climbing support line intersect to form the triangle. These meet at the apex.

The commodity price usually bounces between the trend lines towards the apex before breaking out towards the preceding trend. To confirm the pattern, you must examine various aspects depending on the pattern's direction. If the pattern is preceded by a downtrend, pay attention to a break that occurs beneath the support line.

The pattern usually ends when the stock price finally exits the triangle, so look for a volume increase in the direction of the breakout.

Triangle Ascending

This bullish pattern suggests that the price will end higher. The pattern is formed by two trend lines, one flat line that acts as resistance and one rising line that acts as price support.

The rising support line, which indicates that sellers have begun to exit the security, is the most significant part of the pattern. After the seller's exit the market, buyers proceed to push the price past the resistance level, resuming the upward trend.

Triangle Descending

This is an unequivocal bullish signal. It indicates that when the pattern is completed, the price will fall. The pattern is formed by a flat support line intersecting with a downward sloping resistance line. The pattern indicates that buyers are attempting to raise the price but are encountering significant resistance. After numerous attempts, they eventually fade due to sellers outnumbering them, causing the price to fall.

107

Pennants and flags

This is a group of continuation lines that are very similar to one another. The only difference is in the pattern's consolidation periods. The flag is shaped like a rectangle, while the pennant is shaped like a triangle.

When a spiky price movement is followed by a slanting price movement, the patterns form. The pattern is complete when a price breakout occurs in the same direction as the spike.

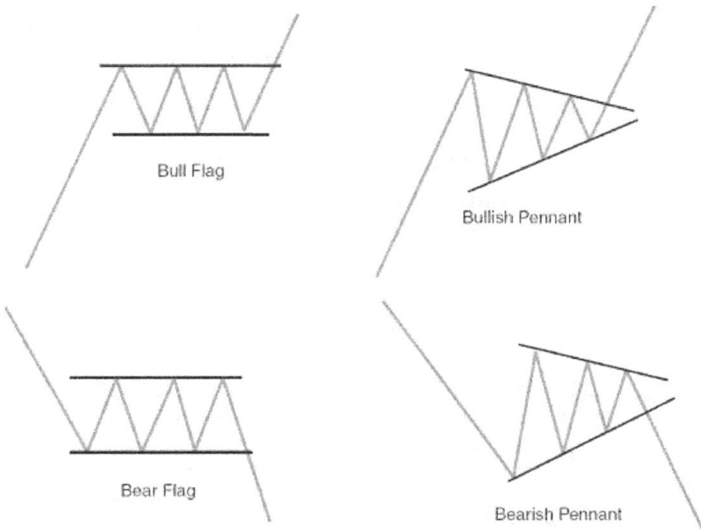

The movement is the result of a large price shift, market consolidation, or a pause before the resumption of an initial trend.

The National Anthem

This section of the pattern creates a rectangle-like pattern.

This rectangle appears as a result of two parallel trend lines pushing the price until it breaks out.

When the price moves through two levels in the previous direction, a buy or sell signal is formed. Always consider the volume when justifying the signal.

108

The Penalty

This is a triangle, with the lines forming a sort of convergence.

The Corner

This chart pattern depicts the reversal of movement that occurs within the wedge. Because it has two trend lines depicting resistance and support, the structure is similar to a symmetrical triangle.

This pattern, however, differs from the triangle in that it lasts longer, typically 3 to 6 months. Unlike typical triangles, the converging trend lines incline upward or downward.

Wedges are classified into two types: falling and rising. The slant distinguishes the two, with a falling wedge slanting downward and an easing wedge slanting upward.

Falling Wedge: This bullish pattern indicates that the price will most likely break through the wedge and move upwards. Look at the resistance trend line, which should have a steeper slope than the support trend line. The buy signal forms for this construction when the price passes through the resistance.

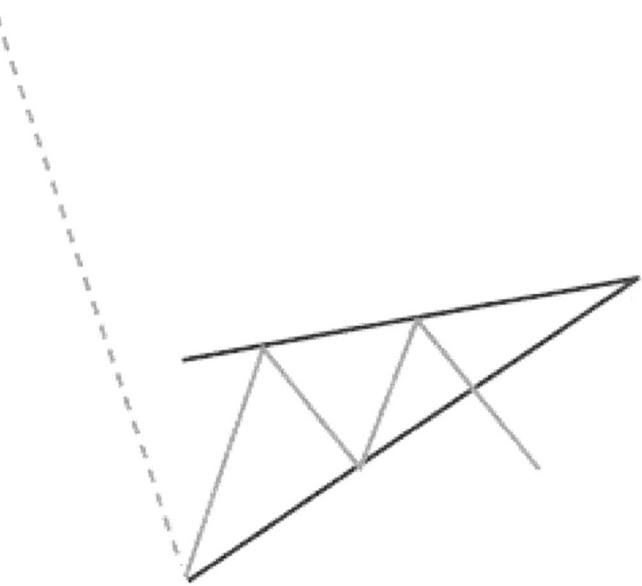

Rising wedge: This is the inverse of the falling wedge in that it has a bearish pattern that indicates that the security may be heading downward. The trend lines that make up this pattern usually converge, with all of them slanting upward.

CHAPTER 18:

TECHNICAL INDICATORS

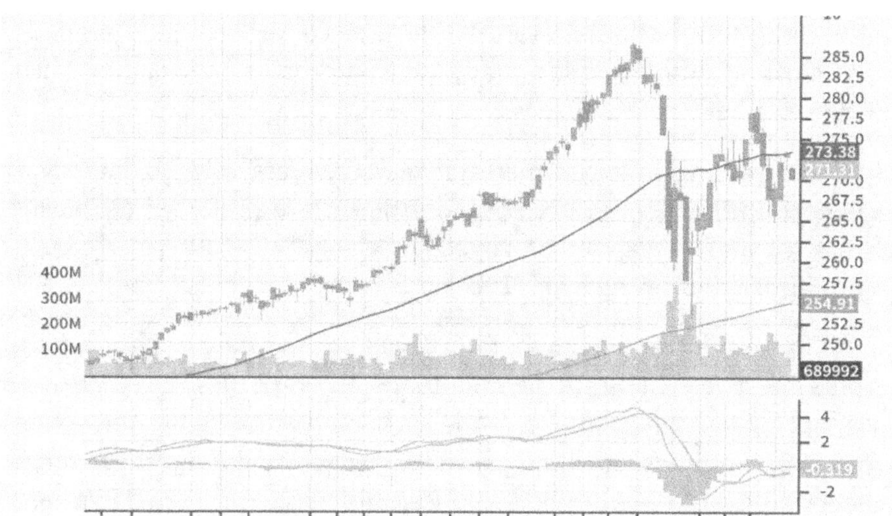

Technical indicators are tools that assist traders in performing technical analyses on stock charts. Learning how to use technical indicators is a very important skill for day trading; without it, you will not be able to become a successful day trader. If you want to win medals in competitive cycling events, you must first learn to ride a bicycle.

Fortunately, technical indicators are simple and easy to learn, and anyone can find a variety of online resources that explain what they are and how to use them.

You can also learn technical analysis by attending offline workshops or lessons. Day traders use dozens of technical indicators, either alone or in combination. The good news is that all technical indicators assist in some way in detecting price movement and indicating appropriate trade entry and exit points.

Day traders choose technical indicators that they like and are comfortable using. It is possible to become obsessed with technical indicators and try to use too many of them for chart analysis. However, it is best to use only a few indicators and stick to them for your trade analysis.

Using too many indicators can lead to confusion and a jumble of crisscrossing lines on your chart. When it comes to using technical indicators, keeping it simple is best.

For trading in stock markets, many traders rely on identifying support and resistance levels. Support levels are preferred for buying, while resistance levels are preferred for selling. This is also referred to as "buying low and selling high."

These are the most important levels to be aware of on charts to trade effectively. Different methods for determining these levels are used depending on market trends. In the stock market, there are three types of trends: uptrends, downtrends, and sideways trends (also called range-bound trends). In an uptrend, the price continues to rise; in a downtrend, the price falls regularly. A sideways or range-bound trend, on the other hand, sees the price move up and down within a horizontal range. A slanting trend line depicts the trading pattern in both up and downtrends.

Lines of Trend

The trend-line is the first tool we'll discuss. This is the most fundamental analysis tool you will ever encounter. I can almost guarantee that you will find this tool in almost any trading software available.

So, what exactly is it?

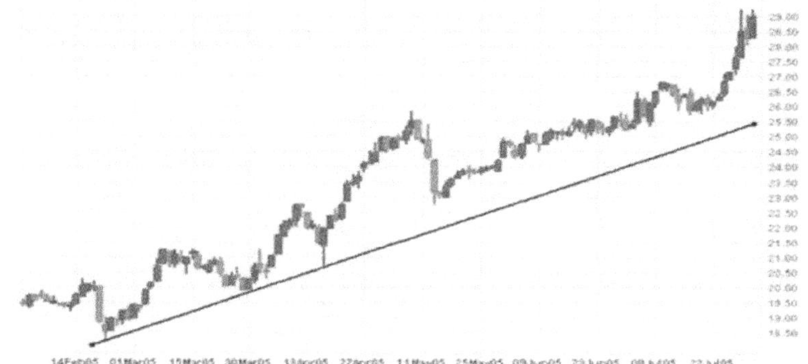

Trend lines are classified into two types based on market direction: uptrend lines and downtrend lines. Let's take a look at each of them individually.

An upward trend line

As the name implies, this is a line drawn on an upward trend, such as the one shown above.

In case you didn't know, an uptrend is simply an upward market movement. When a market rises to form an uptrend, it does so in a zigzag pattern comprised of small troughs and hills.

The troughs are also known as support levels. Levels of support are also known as reactions or corrections. These are the points at which the market retraces its steps before resuming its original course. These troughs provide excellent purchasing opportunities.

When drawing an uptrend line, these troughs become the touching points.

One thing to keep in mind is that the number of touching points on the line must be at least three for it to be considered a valid trend line.

113

A-Line of Decline

Then there's the downtrend line.

Similarly, when a market is falling, it will move in a zigzag pattern, as shown above, creating hills and troughs. This line, unlike the uptrend line, is drawn across the hills. These are also known as resistance points or resistance levels. In addition, they provide excellent selling opportunities in a declining market.

Averages of Movement

Moving Averages are slanted indicators that move along with the trend line and highlight major support and resistance areas. These indicators are divided into different periods, such as 20 days, 50 days, 100 days, and 200 days. When markets are trending, day traders use moving averages to find support and resistance points. A sideways trend, on the other hand, is caused by a horizontal movement of price. In such trends, traders must be aware of horizontal support and resistance levels to buy and sell. In range-bound market conditions, day traders use pivot levels or Fibonacci levels to identify support and resistance. These are the most basic indicators. Certain methods are used to calculate pivot levels, and pivot calculators are freely available online. On technical charts, Fibonacci levels are drawn from the highest and lowest price points. All trading charts allow you to draw Fibonacci levels. The RSI (Relative Strength Index) is the third most important and simplest trading indicator. This indicator, as the name implies, indicates the strength of any trend. The

114

RSI is plotted beneath the main charting area and rises and falls in tandem with the price. A rising RSI indicates the strength of an uptrend, while a falling RSI indicates the strength of a downtrend. It has top and bottom areas, which are referred to as overbought and oversold. Day traders look to sell near the overbought zone and buy near the oversold zone.

One can plan their trading strategies for buying and selling by combining support and resistance indicators with the RSI.

Indicators of Movement

Momentum indicators indicate the strength of a trend and whether or not a reversal is likely. They are extremely useful for locating peaks and troughs. As such, they can assist in determining when and where to enter or exit a trade.

Momentum indicators include the Average Directional Index (ADX), the Relative Strength Index (RSI), and the Stochastic.

These indicators are in the lead.

Market cycles and oscillators

These are indicators that reflect ambiguous price trends, such as the Relative Strength Index (RSI) and the Moving Average Convergence Divergent (MACD). The signals oscillate between upper and lower bounds, and the subsequent readings provide the day trader with information about market conditions.

CHAPTER 19:

TYPES OF TRADES

Some traders prefer forex to the stock market for a variety of reasons. Forex leverage is one of them.

The entire system is completely different when it comes to forex trading. You must first open a forex trading account before you can use leverage. That is the only requirement available, nothing else. You can easily use the leverage feature when you open a forex account. If you trade in the United States of America, you will be limited to a leveraging of 50:1. Outside of the United States, countries are limited to a leverage ratio of about 200:1. It is preferable to be outside of the United States rather than within the United States.

Differences in liquidity

When you decide to trade stocks, you end up purchasing the company's shares, which can range in price from a few dollars to hundreds of dollars. Typically, market prices are influenced by supply and demand.

Trades that are paired

When you trade forex, you are entering a world unseen in the stock market. Though a country's currency fluctuates, there is always a large supply of currency available for trade.

This means that the world's major currencies are typically very liquid. When you trade forex, you will notice that currencies are usually quoted in pairs. They are not quoted in isolation.

This implies that you should be concerned about the economic health of the country in which you have decided to trade. The value of the currency is influenced by the country's economic health. The fundamental considerations differ from one forex market to the next. If you decide to buy Intel stock, your main goal will be to see if the stock's value will rise. You're unconcerned about the prices of other stocks. If, on the other hand, you have decided to sell or buy forex, you must first examine the economies of the countries involved in the pairs. You should find out if the country has better job opportunities, GDP, and political prospects. To make a successful trade in the Forex market, you will need to analyze not one, but two financial entities. In many countries, the forex market tends to be more sensitive to upcoming economic and political scenarios. It is worth noting that, in contrast to many other stock markets, the US stock market is not overly sensitive to foreign events.

Sensitivity of Prices to Trade Activities

When we look at both markets, we can't help but notice that price sensitivity varies when it comes to trade activities.

If a small company with fewer than ten thousand shares has ten thousand shares purchased from it, it could have a significant impact on the stock price. When a large company, such as Apple, buys such a large number of shares, the stock price does not change. When you look at forex trades, you will notice that trades worth a few hundreds of millions of dollars do not affect the major currency. It would have a negligible impact if it did.

Access to the Market

Unlike its counterpart, the stock market, the currency market is simple to enter. It is not easy to trade stocks every second of the day, five days a week in the twenty-first century.

Many retail investors end up trading through a US brokerage that uses a single major trading period per day, which runs from 9: 30 AM to 4:00 PM. They proceed to have a minute trading hour after that time, and this period has price and volatility issues, which discourages many retail traders from using such time. Forex trading is unique. Because there are so many forex exchanges around the world, and they are constantly trading in one time zone or another, such trading can be done at any time of day.

Options Trading vs. Forex Trading

A trader may believe that the US dollar will improve in value when compared to the Euro, and if the predictions are correct, the trader will profit.

CHAPTER 20:

SETUPS AND TRADING STRATEGIES

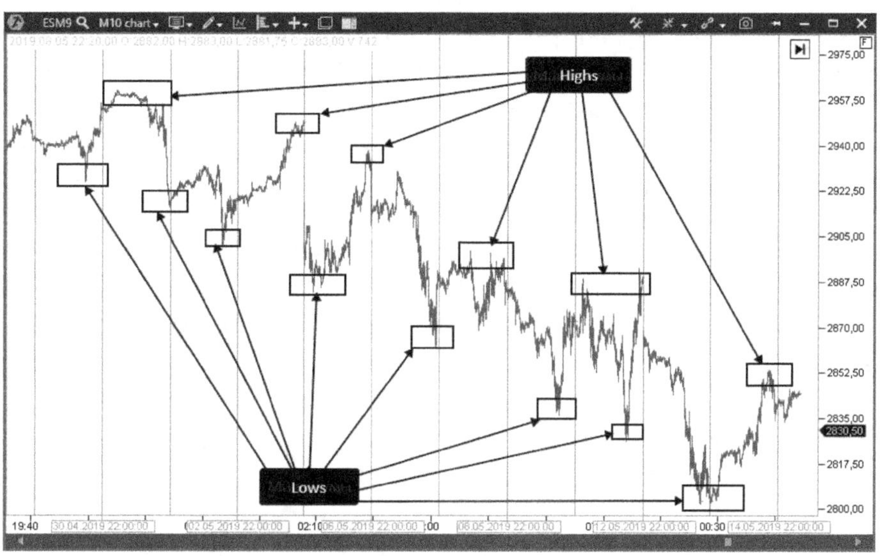

Anyone who wants to make money with stock trading should develop a better strategy for predicting the trend in stock prices to maximize profits. The charts depict trends with various patterns that a newcomer to the trade cannot easily interpret. The patterns in the trend have meanings that give the trader signals on when to make a move by buying or selling stock.

The ABCD Sequence

This is a harmonic pattern from which the other trade patterns are derived. This pattern consists of three swings formed by the AB and CD lines, also known as the legs. The line BC is referred to as the correction line. Lines AB and CD are nearly the same sizes. The AB-CD pattern employs a downward trend, indicating that the reversal will be upward.

119

The bearish pattern, on the other hand, makes use of the uptrend, implying that there will be a downward reversal at some point. When trading with this pattern, you must be aware of the trend's direction and market movement. The ABCD pattern is classified into three types: the classic ABCD pattern, the AB=CD pattern, and the ABCD extension.

When using this pattern, keep in mind that the trade can only be entered once the price has reached point D. As a result, it is critical to examine the chart at the lows and highs; you can use the zigzag indicator to identify swings on the chart. Keep an eye on the price that forms AB and BC as you explore the chart.

C should be on the lower side of A in a bullish trade ABCD. Point A, on the other hand, should be intermediate-high following point B, which is at a low point. D should be a new lower-than-B point. As previously stated, the entry point is at point D; however, once the market reaches point D, you should not be too quick to enter the trade; instead, consider other techniques that would ensure that the reverse is up when it is a bullish trade, and down when it is a bearish trade.

Momentum in the Flag

There are times in a trading market when things are going well and traders are enjoying an upward trend, which results in a chart pattern that resembles a bull flag pattern. It gets its name from the fact that when you look at the chart, it forms a pattern that looks like a flag on a pole.

Because the market is in an uptrend, the pattern is referred to as a bullish flag. The bull flag pattern is distinguished by the following characteristics: the pole is formed when the stock makes a positive move with a relatively high volume, and the flag is formed when the stock consolidates on a lighter volume at the top. The stock is still moving at a relatively high volume, having broken through the consolidation pattern. The bull flag momentum trading strategy is a versatile trading strategy that can be applied to any time frame. The bull is only used to scalp price movements on two occasions of time frame: the second and fifth minute time frames. Trading bull flags also work well when trading on daily charts and can be used effectively when swing trading.

It is simple to trade, but it is difficult to find the exact bull pattern. This issue can be solved by using scanners to look for stocks that are on an upward trend and wait for them to be in a consolidation position at the top. Finviz and chart mill are the best and free scanners for locating bull flags. Some hints can be used to identify a bull flag. When there is an increase in stock volume influenced by news, and stock prices remain high, indicating a clear pattern for a pullback. At this point, you can look for price breakouts above the consolidation pattern or on large volumes of stock. Place a stop order at the bottom of the consolidation to make a move. At this point, the risk-to-reward ratio is 2:1, and it is the best time to target. The volume of the stock is the most significant part of the pattern, and it is a good sign that there will be a significant move and a successful breakout. On the trend, it is also useful to look at the descending trend because it indicates the next breakout. This can be seen in the trend line at the very top of the flag.

Bull flags are useful trading tools when used correctly; however, things can go wrong, so one must be prepared with an exit strategy. There are two strategies: one is to place a stop order below the consolidation area, and the other is to use a moving average that is monitored for the next 20 days. If the stock price falls below the moving average within 20 days, it is time to close the position and explore other trading options.

Trading in Reversals

Reversal trading, also known as a trend reversal pattern, is a trading strategy that signals the end of one trend and the beginning of another.

This pattern appears when the price level of stock has reached its maximum in the current trend. This pattern indicates the possibility of a trend change and the value of price movement.

A pattern formed in an upward trend indicates that the trend is about to reverse and prices will fall soon.

A downward trend, on the other hand, indicates that there will be a cost movement, and it will be upward. To recognize this pattern, you must first understand where specific patterns form in the current trend. At the top of the market, there are distribution patterns; at this point, traders sell more than they buy. Accumulation patterns are those that occur at the bottom of the market, and at this point, traders buy more than they sell. Reversal trends form at all time frames as a result of bank traders either placing trades or profiting from the trades. The trend can be detected when there are multiple fully formed up and down formations; there should be at least two upswings and two downswings, indicating a bearish pattern. The swing highs and lows on the trend line are determined by the reversal pattern that forms. The highs and lows form at similar prices because the bank traders want to appear to be causing a market reversal by getting all of their trades in at the same time. In reality, this isn't the case because they appear at different points along with the trend. As a result, as a trader, you should wait for a bright and steady upward trend to sell in the case of a bullish trade and a bright and steady downward trend to buy in the case of a bearish trade.

There are various kinds of reversal patterns. The double top reversal pattern is characterized by the presence of two tops on the chart. It appears to be "M." The double top pattern has a reversal known as the double bottom pattern, which resembles the letter "W." The double bottom has two bottoms that can be on the same or different supports.

The head and shoulders pattern is another reversal pattern; this pattern resembled two shoulders and ahead. The two shoulders are tops that are slightly lower than the other top, which is called the head. The tops and bottoms of the head and shoulders can also be represented in a descending pattern.

VWAP Investing

The volume-weighted average price is abbreviated as VWAP. When trading in a short time frame, it is a simple and highly effective trading strategy. You must use it for it to work for you.

Different strategies and the most common approach is the waiting for a VWAP cross above and enter long. A VWAP that is above the horizontal line indicates to traders that buyers are entering the market and that prices will rise. Bearish traders may short a stock, causing it to cross below the VWAP, signaling buyers to exit the market and take profits. VWAP can also be used as a resistance or support level to determine trade risk; when the stock trades above the VWAP, the VWAP is used as a support level; when the stock trades below the VWAP, the VWAP is used as a resistance level. In both cases, the VWAP guides the trader in determining when to buy and when to sell.

When conducting trading transactions, trading costs are calculated by comparing the transaction price to a reference or benchmark, the most common of which is the VWAP. The daily VWAP benchmark encourages traders to spread their trades over time to avoid the risks of trading on the day's extreme prices. Because delays and passive trading incur an opportunity cost, this trading strategy favors those who trade with market orders rather than limit orders.

CHAPTER 21

STEP BY STEP TO A SUCCESSFUL TRADE

Typically, over 8,000 stocks are listed in the US stock market, but a typical day trader has access to only a fraction of them because they fail to build a fortune due to a lack of an effective trade strategy. They enter the market based on rumors and leave empty-handed. More often than not, they play at the expense of their valuable capital. Winning in the stock market can be difficult if you lack discipline as a trader. You must identify the right stocks to create a winning situation for yourself. Despite the presence of a learning curve, the effort required to identify the correct stock is worthwhile.

In this chapter, I will walk you through the various steps involved in the successful completion of a trade.

Choosing a Broker

When it comes to choosing brokers, you have a lot of options. There are full service, discounts, online, and other options. Understanding the differences between them and choosing the ones that are best suited to your needs is critical if you want to succeed. Another area that many beginners ignore and then pay the price for is the regulations surrounding options trading. There aren't many rules to follow, but they do have significant implications for your capital and risk management strategies.

This chapter will go over everything in detail.

Which Broker Should I Use?

In general, there are two kinds of brokers: discount brokers and full-service brokers. These days, many full-service brokers have discount arms, so there will be some overlap. A full-service organization is one in which brokerage is only a component of a larger financial supermarket.

Other investment options, estate planning strategies, and so on may be recommended by the broker. They will also have an in-house research department that will send you reports to help you trade more effectively.

In addition, they will provide phone support if you have any questions or want to place an order. A full-service broker will become a better organization to network with once you establish a good relationship with them. Every broker appreciates a profitable customer because it aids in marketing. A full-service broker will have good industry relationships and can put you in touch with the right people if you have specific needs.

The cost of all of these services is that you will pay higher commissions than the average. It is up to you to determine whether this is a reasonable price to pay. As a result, to trade successfully, you do not need to sign up with a full-service broker. Order matching is done electronically these days, so it's unlikely that a person on the floor can get you a better price.

As a result, a full-service firm will not provide you with better execution.

Discount brokers, on the other hand, are all about narrowing their focus. They only assist you in trading. They will not give advice, at least not on purpose from a business standpoint, and phone ordering is non-existent. That does not imply that customer service will suffer as a result. Not at all.

Commissions will be lower as well, far lower than what you would pay for a full-service house. The disadvantage of using a discount brokerage is that you will not receive any special product recommendations or solutions that are not related to your speculative activities.

Many people prefer to trade (via a separate account) with the same broker with whom they have their retirement accounts so that everything is kept in-house.

So, which one should you go with? So, if you want to keep your costs as low as possible, go with a discount broker. Only if you want to keep everything in one place should you go with a full-service broker. Otherwise, there isn't much of a difference between the two options these days.

If you have a large amount of capital, more than half a million dollars, you can make an exception. In these cases, a full-service broker will be less expensive due to volume-based commission offers. You will pay the same rate or a rate that is as close to what a discount broker would charge you, and you will receive all of the additional services. Any additional funds you require for investment can be handled by the firm's wealth management division.

Creating Your Watch List

There is a clear distinction between a watch list and a portfolio.

Before you begin, you should understand that a portfolio is a collection of stocks that you own at any given time, whereas a watch list displays the securities that you own as well as those that you have chosen even if you do not have any investment in them. Watch lists provide insight into the stocks that you may want to add to your personalized portfolio in the future. You should make watch lists based on current events. You should also use any previous watch lists you have. They would remind you of previous searches and would also assist you in fine-tuning your future searches. Increase the frequency with which you go through the list, as well as plan a personal schedule for how you will go through the list and see if the stock meets your criteria. In the event of a negative signal, delete the stock and redirect your attention to other stocks on your watch list. Begin with the broadest sets and then narrow down your stock as you tailor it to your needs. You can weed out stocks that don't meet your requirements if you know what they are. The important thing is to keep the list up to date. As the stock market reinvents itself every day and hour, you should do the same with your watch list. It is best to keep an eye on stocks that appear to be popular. Keep an eye on the popular stocks' upward and downward trends. You will be able to trim and fine-tune your watch list if you keep an eye on the rise and fall of specific stocks. You will no longer be limited to investing in the stocks of large corporations. Instead, you can create a watch list for small businesses. While creating a watch list, keep an eye on the candlesticks, dojis, and charts. Another factor to keep an eye on is price fluctuation. By collecting liquidity components in stocks and adding scanned stock listings that meet general technical criteria, you can create an effective watch list.

Rescanning the watch list to see which stocks are ready for investment and which should be removed from the list after a while is another important strategy to add to your arsenal. For example, you could say that if a stock's volume has been unappealing for the past few days, it should be removed from your watch list. To free up space on a watch list, deletion is required. The shorter it is, the more easily you will be able to remember it.

Margin

The number of assets you currently have in your account is referred to as your margin. Cash and positions are your assets. The amount of margin you have fluctuates with the market value of your position.

Margin is a critical concept to understand because it is at the heart of your risk management discipline. You will be given a choice when you open an account with your broker. You have the option of opening a cash or margin account. You must open a margin account to trade options. In a nutshell, a cash account does not include leverage, so you can only trade stocks with it. There are no account minimums for a cash account, and if there are, they are quite low. A margin account, on the other hand, is governed by entirely different rules.

To begin with, the minimum balances in a margin account are higher. Most brokers have a $10,000 minimum deposit, and some will even increase this amount based on your trading style. The account minimum does not accomplish anything on its own, but it serves as a sort of commitment for the broker.

Execution

We live in an era of high-frequency trading, and the smallest unit of time in the markets has shifted from seconds to microseconds. Trades are constantly coming in, and the matching engine is constantly matching sellers and buyers. Given the market's speed, it is critical to understand that determining the exact price of an instrument is impossible. As a result, in your risk management strategy, you must account for times of high volatility, when the fluctuations will be greater. For the time being, I want you to understand that just because the price you received differed from what was displayed on the screen does not imply that the broker is incompetent.

128

How can you tell if a broker is incompetent? Customer service and the trading terminal's quality give you access to the best indicators. Your broker is not out to defraud you or trade against you. This is not the case with effects, but we are not discussing effects in this book. So, instead of blaming your broker, look at your systems, assuming the broker has passed basic due diligence. You have many options when it comes to placing orders with your broker. You can place various order types, and each order serves a specific purpose. First and foremost, we have the market order. This is the easiest order to comprehend. When you place a market order, you are instructing your broker to fill your entire order at the best price available on the market.

Unless there is some kind of volatility event going on, a market order usually results in faster fills. The limit order is the next type of order you can place. The limit favors order price over order quantity. For example, if you want to buy 100 units of an instrument for $10, your broker will buy as much as possible for less than or equal to $10. If they can only sell 90 units for less than $10, that's it. A limit order is useful for many traders who want to enter a position. The size of the position has a significant impact on directional risk management, so it is critical not to exceed the position limit. This is a beneficial order for such traders. The last type of order you'll come across is a stop order. The stop places a premium on quantity over price.

Stop orders are associated with a trigger, and when the market price hits the trigger, the entire quantity of the order is executed, regardless of the price. Stop orders are extremely useful for quickly exiting positions. The stop-loss order is, indeed, a stop order, with the 'losses' in the name simply referring to the minimization of losses if the trade goes bad. Another type of order to be aware of is the Good Till Cancelled or GTC. The Day order is a relative of the GTC. These two have less to do with order types and more to do with order expiry conditions. A GTC is valid until the trader cancels it explicitly, whereas an order cancels itself at the end of the market session.

Overall, your average broker provides you with over a hundred different types of orders. Do not become bogged down in attempting to figure them all out. The majority of them are used by institutional traders for specific strategies. You don't have to understand a single word of what those orders are about to trade well. Stick to the ones listed here, and you'll be able to trade successfully.

CHAPTER 22:

NEXT STEPS FOR BEGINNER TRADERS

DAY-TRADING SUCCESS IS LARGELY DEPENDENT ON THREE ESSENTIAL SKILLS:

Critical Analysis - You must assess the tension between sellers and buyers and place your money in the winning group.

Financial Management - You must practice excellent money management or you will lose your money in no time.

Self-discipline - You must be extremely disciplined and stick to your trading plan. You must avoid becoming overly depressed or excited in the financial markets, as well as the temptation to make decisions based on your emotions.

131

After reading this book, you should be in a better position to decide whether or not day trading is the right career for you.

Remember that day trading necessitates a certain mindset, discipline, and a set of skills that you will need to hone in the long run.

It is worth noting that many successful day traders are also avid poker players. They claim to enjoy the game's stimulation and speculation.

But keep in mind that a poker is a form of gambling. Daytrading is not because it is based on scientific principles. It necessitates skill, discipline, and other abilities that have nothing to do with luck, such as gambling. Selling and buying financial instruments is a serious business. You must be able to make quick decisions without hesitation or emotion. Failure to do so could result in a significant loss of money as well as depression in some people who do not yet have a formidable mind.

Once you've made up your mind and decided to start day trading, the next step is to get properly educated. You should never begin your day-trading career with real money. Look for brokers who will let you play with simulated accounts while using real market data.

Some day-trading brokers will provide access to an account that uses delayed market data. This is not the best simulator to use. You must work with real-time data to make informed decisions.

The majority of simulated data software is a premium tool, so you will need to budget for it. Avoid free trials because many of them are low-cost platforms. Remember, if you pay peanuts, you get monkeys. Invest in your education, and education in day trading has an upfront cost.

Assume you want to get your master's degree.

This goal will most likely cost you at least $40,000, if not more.

Similarly, many diploma or post-graduate programs will cost significantly more than the education required for your day-trading career.

When you have a simulated account, you must devise your strategy. Try the day-trading strategies we discussed in this book. Ideally, you should become an expert in just one strategy. The most simple day trading strategies are reversal strategies, resistance or support, and VWAP.

You only need to master a few trading strategies to be profitable in this career. Keep it simple. Once you've mastered a solid strategy, make sure to keep your emotions at bay when making a trade.

Continue practicing with the amount of money that you will trade in an actual account. It is simple to buy a $50,000 position on a simulated platform and watch half of it vanish in a matter of minutes. However, do you have the fortitude to lose this much money in real life?

If you answer no, you will most likely become overly emotional while trading and make rash decisions that will result in significant losses. As a result, always trade with the same position and size that you would use in a real account. Otherwise, trading in a simulator is pointless. After training with a simulator, you can transfer to a real account and start with small amounts of real money. Limit the number of trades you do if you are still learning or do not feel emotionally prepared. Continue your self-education, and don't forget to consider your trading strategy.

Do not stop learning about day trading and the market in which you want to participate - equities, forex, ETFs, or futures. These financial markets are quite volatile. Day trading is not what it was a decade ago, and it will not be in the next decade.

So, keep reading and discussing your performance and progress with other day traders. Learn how to plan ahead of time and maintain a forward-thinking attitude. Read as much as you can, but keep an open mind about everything you come across, including this book.

Ask probing questions and don't take 'expert insights' at face value. You should ideally join a day trading group or community. It can be extremely difficult to trade alone. It can also be emotionally draining. It will be extremely beneficial for you to join a day trading community where you can ask questions, discuss options, learn new strategies, and receive alerts and hints about the financial markets.

But don't forget that you must also contribute.

It is important to note, however, that if you are part of a day trading community, you must not always follow the pack. Attempt to develop your ability to think for yourself.

People, in general, change once they become part of a crowd.

They become more impulsive, unquestioning, and always on the lookout for a 'guru' whose trades they can emulate. They react with the crowd rather than with their minds. Day-trading groups may benefit from some trends together, but they may lose if the trends reverse. Don't forget that profitable day traders can think for themselves.

Learn to use your discretion when deciding whether or not to pursue a trade.

CHAPTER 23:

THE BASIC TIPS FOR BEGINNER'S DAY TRADING

It's time to examine how the day trading process works. You could just jump in blindly, but that is a recipe for disaster. Instead, let us get you started on the right track with day trading.

The first question to ask yourself is how much money you intend to invest in your day trading efforts. You must consider not only how much money you are willing to invest, but also how much time you have available. Many investors see day trading as an escape from their regular jobs, while others see it as a solution to the job market's uncertainties. While you may aspire to be a full-time day trader, people can succeed as part-time day traders while working a full-time job.

Beginners should also spend some time simulating investments to get a sense of how comfortable they are with the process and how much talent they possess. It is not a good idea to simply jump in. You must understand the investment market, learn to look for indicators that indicate stock movement, and capitalize on your opportunities.

Infrastructure Issues

While it may seem insignificant, investing time in your workspace and technology can be well worth it. Day trading can be stressful, so having a work area that is quiet and private can be beneficial. Do not underestimate the value of a dependable internet connection and a backup method of controlling your investments if your network fails. Nowadays, it is simple to have a fast land-based internet connection as well as the ability to use your smartphone as a wireless hotspot if your main connection fails. When you have a large investment at stake, it only takes one network failure to convince you of the importance of having a backup internet access plan.

Market Understanding

It's one thing to say you want to invest in stocks; it's quite another to do so. It's another thing entirely to figure out which stocks you should be investing in. Investors divide the market into sectors such as "retailers," "manufacturers," "utilities," "airlines," "energy," "health care," and others. Day traders can choose to target all of these industries or specialize in one or more. As a beginner, concentrating on one industry may be advantageous, especially if it is one with which you are already familiar. Because, as a day trader, you are looking for opportunities for small changes in stocks rather than long-term growth. This means you'll need a lot of money. According to Securities and Exchange Commission (SEC) rules, day traders in the United States must have a minimum of $25,000 in their trading account. This means you'll need at least $30,000 to have some wiggle room. Keep in mind that in the United States, you can currently leverage your trading capital by up to 400%.

This means that with your $30,000, you could control $120,000 in stock. As you already know, this means you could lose four times as much money on your investments. You should be aware that if you do not maintain your maintenance margin amount, you may also receive a margin call. It is preferable to have more funds available when planning your trading account, as this will allow you to consider more stocks. Remember that it is usually more cost-effective to buy shares in multiples of 100, which means that a small investment kitty will either limit you to low-cost stocks or make buying stocks in smaller increments less cost-effective. If you can put more money into your trading account, you will be able to pursue more opportunities and recover from losses.

How to Calculate a Simple Moving Average

A moving average is a basic tool for investing or monitoring the behavior of a stock over a set period. The investor simply adds the closing price of the stock for a given period (two weeks, a month, a quarter, etc.). The number is then divided by the number of trading days in that period. A trader will compute a short-term moving average and a long-term moving average for a stock (you will most likely compute several more to get a better sense of the stock's behavior). A simple moving average can tell you whether a stock is trending upward or downward.

Many traders pay attention when the short-term moving average rises above or falls below the long-term moving average. A short-term moving average crossing above a long-term moving average frequently indicates that the stock is about to enter an uptrend.

The inverse is also true.

137

One method of employing moving averages compares a specific short-term moving average (50 days) to a specific long-term moving average (200 days). When the 50-day moving average falls below the 200-day moving average, you have a bearish signal. This is referred to as the "Death Cross." If the 50-day moving average moves above the 200-day moving average, it is a bullish signal known as a "Golden Cross." While it would be ideal to be able to rely solely on such a simple system, keep in mind that relying solely on a moving average approach is unreliable. It is preferable to use this information as an additional piece of information when making trading decisions.

Selecting a Broker

After you've decided on your trading allocation, you must select a broker or brokerage. The novice investor can choose from several online discount brokers. Many will try to sell you their electronic trading system. Expect to receive offers for free trades and a bonus for choosing their firm. Free trades and cash bonuses are nice, but make sure you choose a broker with whom you feel comfortable and who matches the results of your research. TD Ameritrade, Scott Trade, Fidelity Brokerage, Charles Schwab, Options Express, Merrill Edge, Robin Hood, Loyal3, Options House, E-Option, and others are among the largest online brokerages. Some, such as Robin Hood, offer free trades in exchange for charging interest on margin accounts and using customer cash to earn interest. Others may provide more services or access to a broader range of investment exchanges. Personal advice, on the other hand, is not available from any of these discount brokerages. That is the traditional broker's domain. Consider the cost of trades, your comfort level with the trading program, and your ability to access the company's website when selecting a broker. In addition, look into what others are saying about the brokerage and whether it handles the investment vehicles you want to trade.

Buy and Sell Orders, as well as Set a Stop Loss Price

A trader's every move does not have to be executed immediately or at random. You can instruct your brokerage firm that you only want to buy or sell a stock when it reaches a certain price. Of course, the risk is that the stock will not reach that price while you have money set aside for it. You should also consider establishing a "stop-loss price." This is a precautionary measure to avoid being badly burned if the stock price moves in the wrong direction. Assume you purchased shares of XYZ Corporation at $4.50 per share.

Based on your research, you anticipate an increase in the share price and intend to sell when it reaches $4.75 per share (always plan an exit price). Then something bad happens. When bad news upsets the market (in general or about your stock in particular), your stock price begins to fall instead. You wisely left a stop loss order with your broker, effectively instructing the broker to sell your shares automatically if their price falls to a certain point (perhaps $4.35 in this example) to limit your loss. You should be aware that stop-loss orders are not perfect. At that point, your broker must still find someone to buy the shares. In times of crisis, share prices can fall so quickly that they blow past the stop loss price and continue to fall before finally selling, causing your loss to be greater than anticipated. While this is not a common occurrence, it can be caused by unanticipated events. Because of the price markup, the company selling the Epi-Pen recently saw its valuation drop by $3 billion in a short period. No day trader could have predicted this news, and even with stop-loss orders, traders who expected this stock to rise lost more than they expected.

Why Is Day Trading the Best Way to Increase Your Investing Profits?

Day trading is one of the most effective ways to make money in the stock market and other securities. Many people are looking for a way to make a good profit, and none will find a better option than day trading. Day trading, unlike some of the other methods available, is unique in that you can begin earning profits on your first day.

139

While other traders may have to wait months or even years to see a profit, a day trader can enter the market and make a lot of money in a short period.

CHAPTER 24:

DO'S AND DON'TS OF DAY TRADING

A haphazard approach to day trading is doomed to fail.

Day trading knowledge is a lifelong process, not a one-day event. Profiting from day trading is difficult, especially for beginners who lack discipline and consistency.

Regardless of how difficult this venture is, some practices can help you increase or decrease your profit margins. It is critical for newcomers to this industry to understand the dos and don'ts of day trading. Although there is no guarantee that these factors will ensure your success in day trading, they will assist you in avoiding trouble to some extent. Unlike other businesses, making the right decisions in day trading has an almost immediate impact because even a minor error can cost you a lot of money. Whereas in other business ventures, human emotion is not a critical factor, day trading success is heavily reliant on it. To succeed here, you will need to change your way of thinking and even let go of old habits.

Before entering the trading market, it is critical to understand the risks involved. There is no amount of knowledge or research that can make you guess the specifics of day trading. The best way to learn day trading tricks is to get started. Whether you are already in it or are considering getting into it, here are some of the Dos and Don'ts you should be aware of before entering the trade.

TRADING DO'S AND DON'TS

Make a Trading Strategy

A trading plan is essential for both experienced traders and newcomers to the market. Your plan should include all of the specifics and aspects of your trading strategy. Without a well-thought-out plan, your venture will be more akin to gambling than trading. To accomplish this effectively, seek advice from experienced stock traders on how to create a good trading plan.

Consider yourself a realist.

Always be realistic about the profits you can expect from the trade market. Don't let greed cause you to throw away your good fortune. Because stock markets are volatile and competitive, it is better to accept small profits rather than lose everything. If you miss an opportunity, don't beat yourself up; instead, wait for the next one to come your way. A small profit or gain boosts your confidence in the stock market.

A Strict Routine Is Required

Trading can be a lonely endeavor when you don't have a boss to tell you what to do or what not to do. As a result, sticking to a strict routine will help you overcome the challenge of self-discipline. If you find it difficult to stick to a strict trading schedule, your career as an independent trader may be doomed. As a result, self-discipline is an essential character trait for anyone looking to succeed in the day trade.

Never, Ever Stop Learning

Knowledge exhaustion is something no human being can or has ever done. Even though there are numerous quick learning systems available for new traders, learn the art of day trading from the ground up.

It will increase your chances of success. You must learn the trade through your interpretation rather than from others. Even though various trading strategies that have worked for others may work for you, market conditions vary. You will gain more confidence in your trading abilities as a result.

Seek Professional Help Whenever Possible

To be successful in day trading, you must adhere to a specific coaching program. This reduces the amount of time available for exploration. Even though experimenting is a good way to learn about day trading, it is also a good idea to seek advice from experienced traders. According to one study, 90% of traders who lose money when they first enter the trading market do not fare well in their careers.

Limit Your Losses

Profits and losses are two of the most important factors in day trading. You can't stay in a business where you're losing money all the time. As a result, you must establish a loss limit. When you've reached your limit, decide whether you want to keep trading or exit the market.

Make use of Macro and Micro Idea Generation

A good marketer recognizes market opportunities quickly.

Because day trading is a highly competitive market, it is critical to always outperform the biases.

Understand the factors to consider when looking for a good opportunity.

The trading market is influenced by both macro and micro factors.

As a result, it is critical to link events, drivers, and indicators affecting the day trade market.

Focus on Fundamental Analysis

As a stock trader, it is critical that you thoroughly research and comprehend your company. Financial information about your company, for example, should be readily available to you. You will be able to determine your company's capability and health status as a result of this. A good investment opportunity is one in which the stock price is trading below the company's intrinsic value. The primary reason why most traders do not rely on fundamental analysis is that most traders only trade for a few days.

Conduct a Technical Analysis

This is done by examining the current stock price and currency. Analyze these factors to gain a better understanding of the stock marketing's potential path. Examine the stock's historical performance as well as its current price. These tools will assist you in determining market trends.

Take Action

Do not be afraid to make a move once you have a good understanding of the market and are confident about your next move. Did you know that timing can make or break your success in the stock market? Regardless of the market's direction, you must set your targets to maximize your profits while limiting your losses.

Always keep your emotions under control.

The fast pace and events of day trading can be exhausting. Its experience can be intense and mentally draining. This will be difficult for a beginner, but once you learn to control your emotions, you will be a successful trader. Greed and fear are the two most fundamental traits that are likely to take control of you.

If you are not alert, the two characteristics will take control of you, and you will most likely fail. Because of fear, do not leave too quickly when everything is going your way. However, do not let it run for too long; if there is a consistent downfall, take your profits before it all runs out.

Have a Boundary

To maximize your profits, follow the golden rule of stop losses and soft limits'. This means that your previous lowest or highest point is close to triggering a stop loss. If the market is moving to a position you predicted, this is the ideal time to let your position move.

The most important thing to remember here is to maximize your profits. The number of commodities and stocks should be kept in check. Every stock is distinct in its way. As a result, you will learn the tricks over time, and your judgment will improve as you gain experience.

Mistakes Are Accepted

Failures and setbacks are the norms of business once you enter the stock market. It is incorrect to believe that only newcomers are prone to making mistakes; even the most experienced stock traders make mistakes. The time of entry or exit in the market is a common mistake made by most day traders. You will be able to predict and execute better as a result of these mistakes. As previously stated, seeking knowledge from experienced traders will help you minimize market mistakes. When you enter the market, you will notice that what you experience differs

145

from what you learned in books. As a result, the best teacher in any stock market is experience.

Take Note of Every Mistake You Make As You Improve

In the stock market, losing trade is not the end of the world.

Instead, view it as a learning opportunity. Contrast what you expected in the market with what you got. Identify the errors you made as well as the underlying factors that may have contributed to your failure.

DOS AND DON'TS OF DAY TRADING

Don't take any big risks.

When it comes to day trading, avoid greed at all costs. Consider the possibility of losing money before taking any risks. If you can't handle the possibility of losing, it's not worth investing your money. Keep in mind that even with the best strategies, the chances of making a profit in the stock market are 50/50. Take the time to learn the specific ratios that apply in the stock market, as they change from time to time.

Don't Invest for Revenge.

As a human being, you are likely to respond with vengeance to an unavoidable failure. Never approach day trading with such a strategy because you will fail miserably. In the event of a failure, take a step back and study to determine the root cause of your failures. Take the time to plan your next move. I can assure you that entering the market with the intent of retaliation will do you more harm than good.

Do not trade too frequently.

It is recommended that you trade once in a while. Only make an investment when a fantastic opportunity presents itself. Before investing in any stock market, you should conduct thorough research.

However, instead of trading, you can spend as much time as you want to analyze the market situation. Stop wasting your time trading because it is a recipe for disaster.

If you are new to the market, you should avoid scalping.

Scalping is nothing more than taking a shortcut by engaging in trades that last only a few seconds. Even though scalping is a good way to make money, it is risky. Understanding and predicting a sudden shift in market movements requires a certain level of skill and experience. You must pay a spread fee on every trade you make, regardless of the direction of the trade.

As a result, experience and knowledge are required because you must earn pips above the spread cost.

It is critical to take notes as you experiment with different strategies. The two most important factors are the stock market, experience, and knowledge.

Do not rely on untrustworthy sources of information.

Frequently, you will receive emails, text messages, or advertisements claiming a large profit on any stock. Not that you should shut down such sources; rather, ensure that the information they provide is authentic and reliable. As a good trader, you must be cautious not to fall into the hands of brokers who are looking for the commotion. These people can easily get you into bad trades, resulting in losses.

Avoid penny stocks at all costs.

Penny stocks should be the last thing you do as a beginner in day trading. Experienced traders will advise you not to enter a trade that is difficult to exit. Also, because penny stocks are highly illiquid, your chances of making large profits are slim.

Do Not Refuse To Retain Your Profits

It is natural for any human being to want more or to never be satisfied with what they have because everyone is in business to make more money. Furthermore, when you want to make quick money, you make a mistake.

As a result, every trader hopes to make unfathomable profits on their first trade. However, in the stock market, what appears to be a huge gain can turn out to be a huge loss. Expecting a large profit from your trade is not a bad thing. However, it is critical to be realistic about the profits you anticipate from your investment.

148

CHAPTER 25:

COMMON DAY TRADING MYTHS YOU SHOULD BE AWARE OF

It is never a good idea to listen to everything you hear in this digital age. Some information on the internet is simply designed to distract you from reality. Other facts are present to deceive you. There are a few myths about day trading that have been around for a long time. Some of these myths are simply stories designed to discourage people from profiting from this lucrative trading activity. If you are new to trading, you must be aware of some of these myths and how to distinguish them from the truth. This section debunks some of the most common day trading myths.

Day trading is comparable to gambling.

One of the most common misconceptions about day trading is that it is similar to gambling. If you mention this to an experienced investor, they are likely to punch you in the face. This is because this myth is false.

Day trading is not a form of gambling. Gambling is entirely based on chance. Trading, on the other hand, will be determined by your logic and reasoning.

You must set aside your emotions to trade successfully.

You should also be aware that there are no quick profits to be had from day trading. Contrary to popular belief, this is what the majority of gamblers anticipate from their gambling activity. You must understand that trading is not the same as gambling. Don't be swayed into thinking this is true.

It's a Man's Sport

If you come across such a myth, don't be surprised. Trading is not something that only men can do. There are a lot of female traders out there. Just because you believe there is a high level of risk associated with day trading does not imply that it is a man's game.

No! Some traders argue that women are the best investors in day trading. As a result, don't make assumptions based on hearsay.

You are going to lose everything.

To be honest, how can you lose everything if you use the risk management techniques discussed in this manual? The majority of people who fail at day trading do so because they enter the market without a plan.

In addition, many of them let their emotions get the best of them. As a result, they make decisions that harm their finances. It's also possible that they lack the discipline to stick to their plans. Having a strategy is not enough to ensure that you limit your losses and increase your profits. You must walk the walk by putting the plan into action.

Stopping Isn't Necessary

Some may lead you to believe that using stops demonstrates that you are too afraid to take risks. This, too, is far from the truth. The truth is that stops are tools that can help save you from losing all of your capital in a single mistake. It is sometimes preferable to live and fight another day. As a result, you must always embrace the concept of using stops.

Trading all day increases your earnings.

You will notice that there are good and bad times to trade based on the various strategies you will employ. As a result, it is irrational to believe that one could make more money trading all day. Most traders prefer to trade in the morning because they can capitalize on high market volatility during these times.

Others prefer to trade at different times of the day. As a result, trading all day does not guarantee that you will make more money. Because there is no guarantee in day trading, you could potentially take on more losses.

Allowing Your Victories to Run

Day traders who are just starting will believe that the best way to profit from their good trades is to let them run. One thing to keep in mind is that you can only make money if you sell the securities you're trading. As a result, letting your victories run is risky. When market prices fall dramatically, anything can happen. It could have been worse if you had taken a break outside, hoping to make a fortune from your investments. As a result, you should always recognize the importance of taking profits when necessary. Don't be avaricious.

Leverage is harmful.

Some traders who have failed in the industry argue that leverage is harmful. Without a doubt, using leverage for the wrong reasons will harm your trading business.

Leverage is essentially a tool that allows you to buy more securities with less money. As a result, if you use a good trading strategy, you could end up making a lot of money thanks to the leverage provided by your trader.

A sizable bankroll is required.

Based on what has been discussed, you will need varying amounts of capital depending on the market you choose to trade-in. This means that the myth of needing a large bankroll to trade does not apply. You can start trading online with as little as $1,000. You should, however, exercise caution when limiting yourself to a specific amount. If you want to earn a good return, you must be willing to take risks.

You don't require any rules.

Another common misconception is that you do not need to follow any day trading rules. Consider the following scenario: a soccer game is played without any rules. This would undeniably be perplexing. Day trading is the same thing. You will only incur losses if you do not follow the rules. Eventually, you will abandon the belief that day trading is ineffective. As a result, you must have rules in place to help you maintain your discipline.

It's important to understand that several myths about day trading can keep you from learning the truth. With some in-depth research into this subject, you will gain a better understanding of the potential benefits that may accrue as you trade. Don't believe everything you hear. Before entering any trading market, make sure you have done your homework.

CHAPTER 26:

COMMON MISTAKES TO AVOID

Focusing on the Fundamentals

When you were first learning the fundamentals of day trading, you most likely focused heavily on the fundamentals when determining which propositions were worthwhile and which were just as likely to result in a loss as again. However, as you continue to hone your skills, it is critical to understand that the fundamentals aren't nearly as important as the market's current trends. Regardless of the individual facts, if the market is trending downward, it affects both good and bad picks. The sooner you begin to see the forest for the trees, the sooner you will begin to make significantly fewer losing trades.

153

Concentrate solely on the signs you see, not on whether or not they correspond to what you expect to happen. Remember, whenever possible, trade mechanically.

Walking Away from an Unoccupied Position

You might have been able to walk away from the action in the middle of an open trade if you were only trading haphazardly. If you want to rise above average, you must train yourself to break that habit right now. Massive price swings can occur in an instant when the major players decide to make a move. As a result, if you decide to go make a sandwich at the wrong time, you may find that your hunger has cost you dearly. Day trading is a high-risk endeavor, and you must learn to treat it as such if you hope to achieve true success in the field.

Instead of Learning, Follow

When you first begin trading regularly, you will most likely want to find a mentor to teach you the ins and outs of day trading with a purpose. This is a fantastic idea, and it comes highly recommended as long as you make proper use of the resources provided by your mentor. This means that, while you should listen to what your mentor says, you should also take the time to learn why certain moves are a good idea, rather than blindly following in your mentor's footsteps. While both can often result in the same amount of financial gain, taking the time to understand both the theory and the practice can eventually lead to a more prodigious output in the long run. You should set a time limit for the amount of time you intend to spend with the potential mentor and work hard to become self-sufficient by that time; any longer, and you may find the experience limiting rather than beneficial.

Restricting Your Options

While focusing on short-term markets will likely result in the most consistent returns, viewing yourself solely as a day trader is a good way to limit your overall investment potential. While it is perfectly acceptable to focus on day trading the majority of the time, being unwilling to venture outside of that time frame will only prevent you from turning a good trade into a great one.

Furthermore, if you are currently working with 5-minute charts, you should consider switching to 30-minute charts. When compared to 1 or 5-minute charts, this does not significantly increase your risk and, in fact, decreases your risk because you can more clearly see where trends are developing rather than simply reacting to noise. If you believe you have a genuine advantage when trading in the 1-minute time frame, do yourself a favor and experiment with a weightier chart for a few days; you will be surprised at how much of a difference it can make.

Following Instead of Learning

As your skills improve, you should become more interested in the overall market trend and less interested in individual scalping trades. While there is money to be made in these scenarios, the odds are roughly the same as winning the lottery and are nowhere near what you can expect to see when you simply use a reliable system at the right times. The choice with the highest probability is correct 100 percent of the time.

Limiting your Options

Limiting yourself to a single market is a recipe for lost profits, just as you should not limit yourself to a specific time frame. While it may seem natural to stick to a single market because it is the one you are most familiar with, if you ever hope to be more than a casual trainer, you must eventually step outside your comfort zone and begin trading based on available opportunities, regardless of the market in question.

155

Remember that whatever program you are using is most likely connected to all markets at the same time, giving you an advantage that many more experienced traders do not have. This is related to learning to recognize global trends, regardless of the market in which they occur; if you follow a positive trend across multiple markets, there's no reason it can't continue to be profitable. Make the most of your research by following your opportunities wherever they may present themselves.

Making Use of a Gimmick

Despite the perfunctory cautionary warnings about the market's inherent volatility, many people continue to believe that they have the magic bullet that will set them apart from the pack. Unfortunately, there are no guaranteed systems or gimmicks for successful day trading. Don't waste time looking for one; instead, invest that time in locating the most dependable system you can find. This will still not result in a guaranteed success rate, because nothing is perfect, but it will be far more worthwhile than chasing a day trader fairy tale.

CHAPTER 27:

THE RULES OF DAY TRADING

Let us now look at some of the day trading rules that every investor should follow. These rules are not always unbreakable. You can choose to follow or ignore these rules as you embark on your investing journey. They should, however, be followed to provide you with the best day trading experience possible from the start of your investing career.

Day trading is a serious endeavor.

When some people first start day trading, they believe it is all for fun and games, and they do not take the profession seriously. This could be a fatal error. While it is important to enjoy what you are doing, it is also important to remember that it is a serious business.

157

Day Trading is a Serious Business

Some types of investing are easier to manage as a side job or on the weekends. If this is the type of investment you are looking for, you should avoid day trading. This type of investing is intended to be a day-to-day business, and many people consider it their day job. This means that if you decide to become a day trader on a formal basis, you must approach it in the same way you would any other career.

You must get up in the morning, prepare for your day, and ensure that you are ready to work by your assigned time, which could be as early as 7 a.m.

While you will have some schedule flexibility from your regular job, which means you can set a later start time in the morning, you will want to make sure to set a schedule that you will follow at least Monday through Friday. Even if you work from home, you should keep distractions to a minimum. You wouldn't want to be focusing on day trading and watching television at the same time, for example. Set up an office for yourself and focus on your work. Prepare for your job as a day trader in the same way you would for any other office job. You should not come to work in your pajamas. If you approach this as a career, you are more likely to feel compelled to give it your all and succeed.

Day trading will not help you become wealthy quickly.

Day trading should not be viewed as a get-rich-quick scheme.

This is a common misconception, and it is one of the reasons why people turn to day trading. If you truly want to be a successful day trader, you must have the patience to build your investments as well as the understanding that it takes time.

Day trading is more difficult than it appears.

Day trading is not as simple as it appears, but that does not mean you should put this book aside and decide not to become a day trader. It simply means that you will need to devote more time to learning about day trading than you anticipated. Before you make your first investment, you should ensure that you are well-versed in the field. Fortunately for you, this is one of the reasons I decided to write this book in the first place. I want to give you a comprehensive beginner's guide so you can learn everything you can about day trading in one place. In other words, I've done the majority of the legwork for you.

Trading is Not the Same as Investing

One of the most important rules to understand before becoming a day trader is that it is not the same as investing. To help you understand the distinction, here are a few key distinctions between trading and investing:

As an investor, you need to know where the stock market is going in the future. However, as a day trader, you only need to be concerned with which stocks will provide you with the greatest financial gain on that particular day. You examine the minutes more closely. You won't even notice the time and won't be concerned about the next day, week, month, or year.

You are not going to win every trade.

No matter how experienced you become as a day trader, you will still have days when you lose a trade. Many people imagine themselves becoming so skilled at trading that they will never make a mistake and will only make money. Every game has its own set of rules and regulations, and day trading is no exception. If you are new to the game, you must remember all of the standard rules that have been put in place to keep the game under control. That being said, it is important to note that these rules are not infallible, but they can be useful in making day trading decisions. There are numerous day trading rules that you must learn, regardless of whether you specialize in forex, stocks, options, cryptocurrency, or futures. Failure to follow some of the rules can result

159

in significant losses. While some rules vary depending on where you are located and the size of your trade, this will focus on the most important rules. Furthermore, it will go over the rules that novices can follow as they enter the complicated world of day trading.

These rules will also help experienced traders improve their trading performance, for example, in the area of risk management.

Beginner's Rules

If you are new to this field, the day trading rules discussed below can help you reap commendable profits while avoiding significant losses.

Enter, Exit, and Escape

One common mistake that newcomers make is entering the arena without a well-thought-out game plan. Do not dare to press the "enter" button unless you have a plan for getting in and out. When you are new to a field, it is natural to feel a sense of excitement. It is important to note, however, that if you do not have a formidable plan, you will be eliminated from the game. Use risk management rules as well as stop-loss orders to reduce losses.

Timing

I'm sure you usually get up bright and early, ready to face the day trading arena. However, avoiding the first quarter-hour after the market opens is arguably one of the most important trading rules to follow.

The majority of the activity at this time involves market orders or panic trades from the previous night. Instead, you should use this time to monitor for reversals. The first quarter-hour is also avoided by the most experienced day traders.

Be Aware of Margin

Do you remember when you were starting and looking for capital? It was very easy to get caught up in the margin.

However, keep in mind that this is a loan. A loan that must be paid back. While it has the potential to significantly boost your profits, it also has the potential to leave you nursing significant losses. As a result, before using margin, it is best to learn how to trade properly.

Accounts for Practice

You have a lot to learn and nothing to lose by taking the initiative to start with a demo account. Because you are being funded by simulated money, you can nurture your craft with plenty of time and space for trial and error. Many brokers will provide you with free practice accounts because they are the best place to learn about strategies, patterns, and charts, as well as the quarter-hour day trading practice.

Recognize and Accept Your Loss

Almost all the veteran traders have achieved their success because they were willing to lose and learn from their mistakes. Accept that losing is merely a means of gaining more experience. That being said, it is also critical to emphasize the importance of cutting your losses.

Observe Everything

A veteran once said that a great trader is similar to an athlete in that he may have the skills, but he must train himself on how to use them.

Complacency should not be something that great traders associate with because it is something that they should always be; I am looking for that edge. This means they use a variety of resources to expand their knowledge. They can make use of anything, including videos, books, blogs, and forums.

Perform a Tip Evaluation

It's natural to get excited when you're given a thought-provoking tip. Nonetheless, unconfirmed tips from untrustworthy sources can result in significant losses. Jesse Livermore, a trader, claims that experience has taught him a tip or a series of tips that will make him more money than his judgment. As a result, double-check any information that may influence your trading decisions.

Risk Management Guidelines

The rules of money management and the risks of day trading are important factors in determining a trader's success. Although you are not required to follow these rules to the letter, they have proven to be invaluable to many.

The 1% Rule of Risk

The goal here is to prevent you from trading beyond your skill level. When you use this technique, whether you have a trade subsidy or not, you will always have some reserve. I have money in the bank to assist you in correcting your balance later on.

The idea is that you should never trade with more than 1% of your total account on a single trade. For example, if you have $50,000 in your account, you will only use $500 on your trade.

CHAPTER 28:

POWER PRINCIPLES TO ENSURE A STRONG ENTRY INTO DAY TRADING OPTIONS

Buy a call option if you think the market will rise

I cannot emphasize this enough: if you want to be successful at day trading options, you must have a plan. Every day, you put your money on the line. I'm sure squandering those hard-earned dollars isn't the intention, but that's exactly what will happen if no proper plan is in place.

Power Principle #1 – Make sure you have good money management.

Money is the fuel that keeps the engine of the financial industry running smoothly. As an options day trader, you must learn to manage

163

your money in a way that works for you rather than against you. It is an important part of risk management and profit maximization.

Money management is the process of allocating funds for spending, budgeting, saving, investing, and other purposes.

Money management is a term that any person with a career in the financial industry, particularly in the options trading industry, is intimately familiar with because this allocation of funds is the difference between a winning and a struggling options trader.

Tips for managing your money are provided below so that you can maintain maximum control over your options day trading career.

Tips for Options Traders on Money Management

Define your short and long-term financial goals so you can see what you want to save, invest, and so on. Make certain that these are recorded and easily accessible. Your trading strategy will assist you in defining your financial objectives.

Create an accounting system. There is a wide range of software available to assist with this, but it doesn't matter which one you use as long as you can keep records and easily track the flow of your money.

To manage your money, use position sizing. The process of determining how much money will be allocated to entering an options position is known as position sizing. To accomplish this effectively, allocate a reasonable portion of your investment fund to individual options. It would be foolish, for example, to spend 50% of your investment fund on one option. That is 50% of your capital that could be lost if you make a loss in that position. A good percentage is to allocate no more than 10% of your investment fund to individual option positions. This percentage allocation will assist you in getting through difficult periods, which will inevitably occur, without losing all of your funds. Never invest money you can't afford to lose.

Allow the emotion to override this principle and cloud your judgment.

Diversifying your portfolio spreads your risks. You diversify your portfolio by investing in different areas, adding to your investments regularly, staying aware of commissions at all times, and knowing when to close a position.

Power Principle #2 – Make certain that the risks and rewards are balanced.

Options day traders should use the risk/reward ratio to determine each and make adjustments as needed to ensure that losses are kept to a minimum and returns are as high as possible. The risk/reward ratio is a calculation that compares profit potential to potential losses. This necessitates an understanding of the potential risks and profits associated with an options trade. A stop-loss order is used to manage potential risks. A stop-loss order is a command that allows you to exit an options trade position once a certain price threshold is reached. Profit is sought after by following a predetermined strategy. The potential profit is calculated by subtracting the entry price from the target profit. This is calculated by dividing the expected return on investment in options by the standard deviation. Diversifying your portfolio is another way to manage risks and rewards. Always diversify your investments across various assets, financial sectors, and geographies.

Develop a Consistent Monthly Options Trading System – Power Principle #3

The goal of doing options trading daily is to have a winning options trading month overall. That will not happen if you trade options infrequently. You can't expect to make a lot of money at the end of the month if you only did two or three transactions. To increase your chances of winning every month, you must trade options regularly. The only way to do so is to create a system in which you trade options at least five days a week.

To have good months consistently, you must develop strong daily systems that keep your overall monthly average high. As a result, developing a daily options trading schedule is critical. Here's an example of an effective options trading day schedule: Conduct market analysis. This must be completed before the markets open in the morning. As a result, the options day trader must get an early start on the day. This includes scanning the news for major events that may affect the markets that day, checking the economic calendar, and analyzing the actions of other day traders to determine volume and competition. Take charge of your portfolio. How an options day trader accomplishes this depends on the strategies that he or she employs, but in general, it is about assessing positions that you already have or are considering for efficient management of entry and exits that day. It also enables good financial management.

Fill out new positions. After evaluating the market and fine-tuning your portfolio, the next step is to place new trades on the same day. This step requires research and sound decision-making. The options trader who had already determined how the market was performing and forecasted for the day's performance would have noticed relevant patterns. The key here is to enter trades regularly using a sound strategy. Keep an eye on the bullish, bearish, neutral, and volatile watch lists and run technical scans to narrow down which positions you want to pursue. Include learning throughout the day. Continuous learning is essential for an options trader, but it does not always have to take the form of formal classes or courses. You can learn more about options and day trading by following mentors, reading books, listening to podcasts, reading blogs, and watching online videos. These types of activities are simple to incorporate into your daily routine. Even a few minutes of study per day can significantly improve your options day trading game while also stimulating your mind.

Maintaining regular contact with other options day traders is another excellent way to expand your knowledge.

Consider a Brokerage Firm That Is Appropriate for Your Level of Options Expertise (Power Principle #4).

When selecting a broker, there are four important factors to consider:

- The prerequisites for establishing a cash and margin account.
- The broker's one-of-a-kind services and features.
- The commissions and other fees are levied by the broker.
- The broker's reputation and level of options expertise.

Let's take a look at each of these individual components and see how you can use them to enhance your options day trading experience.

Cash and Margin Accounts for Brokers

To conduct transactions, every options trader must open a cash account and a margin account. They're just tools for the job. A cash account is loaded with cash and allows an options day trader to conduct transactions. Margin accounts make transactions easier by allowing the borrower to borrow money against the value of the security in his or her account.

A minimum deposit is required for both of these types of accounts. Depending on the broker, this can range from a few thousand dollars to tens of thousands of dollars. When deciding which brokerage firm is best for you, you must be aware of the requirements.

Broker Services and Benefits

Different brokerage firms provide different types of services and features. For example, if an options trader wants to have a personal broker assigned to him or her to handle his or her account, he or she must look for a full-service broker. In this case, there are minimum account requirements that must be met. In addition, commissions and other fees are typically higher with these types of brokerage firms. While the fees are higher, it may be preferable for novice traders to have that full service dedicated to their needs and the learning curve.

If, on the other hand, an options trader does not have the capital required to meet the minimum requirements of a full-service broker or would prefer to be more in control of his or her option trades, a discount brokerage firm is an option. The benefit of discount brokerage firms is that they typically have lower commissions and fees. The vast majority of internet brokerage firms are discount brokers.

Other factors to consider when selecting a brokerage firm include whether or not the broker provides real-time quotes.

- The speed with which claims are processed.
- Bank wire services are available.
- Monthly statements are available.
- Whether written or electronic confirmations are used.
- Other Fees and Commissions

When an options trader enters and exits positions, he or she must pay commissions. Every brokerage firm has its own set of **commission fees**.

These are typically based on the options trader's level of account activity and account size.

Broker Reputation and Options Knowledge

You don't want to be duped out of your money because you chose the incorrect brokerage firm. As a result, you must select a broker with a well-established and long-standing reputation for trading options. You also want to work with a brokerage firm that provides excellent customer service, which can help you lay the groundwork for negotiating lower commissions and allows for flexibility. Options trading is a complex service, and your brokerage firm must be able to assist you when dealing with difficult transactions.

Among the reputable online brokerage firms are:

168

- E*TRADE
- Options button.
- Scottrade
- Ameritrade
- Train Station

Ameritrade Train Station Power Principle #5 – Ensure Automated Exits

Even though I have stated that emotions should be avoided when trading options, we are all human, and emotions will inevitably enter the picture at some point. Given this, systems must be developed to reduce the impact of emotions. Having your exits automated is one step you can take to ensure that emotions are not involved when dealing with options day trading.

Using bracket orders makes this easier.

A bracket order is an instruction given by an options trader when he or she enters a new position that specifies a target or exit and a stop-loss order that corresponds to that. This order ensures that a system is set up to record two points: the profit target and the maximum loss point that will be tolerated before the stop-loss kicks in. Either order's execution cancels the other.

GLOSSARY

Some of the most common trading terms you will encounter while day trading.

A

Ask

The asking price is what a seller offers a buyer for the sale of any financial asset.

B

Broker

A broker is a person or a company who acts as an intermediary between traders and exchanges and receives a commission whenever a trade is executed between these two parties.

Bid

In day trading, the bid price is what a buyer offers to a seller in exchange for the purchase of any financial asset.

Bear

Bear traders are those who have a negative outlook on markets and expect the price to fall.

The Bear Market

The price trend continuously declines in a bear or bearish market.

Bull

Bull traders are those who have a bullish outlook on the market and expect the price to rise.

The market is booming.

Bull Market

A bull market is defined as a market with rising prices.

C

The Cash Market

A market for trading actual stocks and commodities.

Call Option Contracts that are bullish on the market. Day traders adore it.

D

Daily Trading Cap

Every day, exchanges determine the maximum price range for any contract.

The daily trading limit does not mean that trading will be halted, but rather that price movement will be limited.

Order of the Day

An intraday session order that is only valid for that session. When the session ends, it is automatically canceled.

Day Trading

The simultaneous purchase and sale of financial assets. Stocks, commodities, forex, and options are all examples of assets.

Traders who buy or sell financial assets in a single session and close all positions before the end of the day are known as day traders. They do not carry their positions forward to the next session.

E

Exchange

Exchange is a centralized, regulated marketplace where buyers and sellers trade financial assets.

F

Futures

Derivative contracts that cover the purchase and sale of financial assets for delivery in the future. These transactions occur on a futures exchange.

Contract for Futures

These are derivative agreements that take place on a futures exchange. These are legally binding on traders who buy or sell financial instruments intending to deliver them in the future. Futures contracts follow standard rules regarding quantity and delivery time.

G

Valid until Canceled (GTC)

Open orders with instructions to buy or sell at a specific future price can remain open until the order is executed.

H

Hedge

The simultaneous purchase and sale of a futures derivative contract. This is done to balance the profit and loss of open positions in the derivatives and cash markets.

Hedger

Hedgers are companies or individuals who, while holding positions in cash markets, make an opposite trade in the derivatives markets to offset any potential loss.

Hedging

The act of offsetting any potential loss in cash markets by taking an equal but opposite position in derivative markets.

I am the initial margin.

To open a new position in derivative markets, such as futures and options, traders must deposit a minimum amount of money into their trading accounts, known as the initial margin. This is done to reduce the risk of loss due to market volatility. The level of initial margin can rise or fall in response to market volatility.

L

Final Trading Day

The last trading day is the last trading day of derivative contracts, not the last trading day of the month (futures & options). The monthly derivative contracts are settled among traders on this trading day.

A limit order is an order to buy or sell a financial instrument at a specific price that cannot be exceeded. This indicates that the buyer or seller will only trade at a specific price.

Liquidity

A feature of tradable financial instruments that demonstrates their ease of trading. Traders and investors prefer to buy and sell highly liquid assets because they can be bought and sold quickly.

Long

If a trader has a bullish outlook for the market, he is said to be 'long.' When buyers expect the price to rise, they take a long position.

M

Margin of Maintenance

This is the bare minimum that traders must maintain in their trading accounts to keep a position open. The maintenance margin is typically lower than the initial margin.

Call for Margin

If a trader's account falls short of the required maintenance margin, the brokerage firm will contact them and demand that they deposit the required amount. If a trader fails to do so, the brokerage firm liquidates his positions for the same amount.

Order of the Market

An order to buy or sell any financial entity at the current market price. When traders want their trades to be executed quickly, they use this order.

Closed Market

This order is used at the end of a trading session to buy or sell financial assets. The order price is typically within the market's closing range.

O

Price of Offer

It demonstrates the seller's willingness to sell a financial asset at an agreed-upon price. It is also known as the 'Ask' price.

The order is now open.

An order that is not carried out. It can stay open until the specified price is met or the order is canceled.

P

Pit A location on the trading floor where traders conduct their buying and selling activities.

Position

A trade in which the process of buying and selling has not been completed. A free trade.

S

Price of Settlement

On a trading day, this is the last price paid for any financial entity.

This is also referred to as the closing price.

Scalp

A method of day trading in which speculators trade for small profits.

These transactions are completed in a matter of minutes.

175

Scalpers trade multiple times in a single day.

Short

A trader is said to be short on the market if he has a negative or bearish outlook on the market. Also, the selling side of a derivative contract is open.

Speculator

Traders try to predict market movements and price changes to profit.

Spot

Spot markets are used for financial assets that require immediate delivery and payment in cash.

Spread The difference in price between the bid and ask.

Order to Discontinue

Also referred to as a stop-loss order. This order is used by traders to limit their risk of loss or to book profits at a specific price level.

Stop Limitation

Similar to a stop order, but with a slight twist. When the price is at or above the stop price, the stop order acts as a limit order in buying.

When selling, a limit order is formed when the price is trading at or below the stock price.

T

Tick

The smallest increase in the price of any financial asset in trading.

Some scalpers trade using tick price.

CONCLUSION

Technical traders are day traders. They execute trades based solely on chart readings, ignoring factors such as the company's profitability, P/E ratio, debt-to-equity ratio, and so on. Technical charts are the only tools a day trader has for making money.

Day traders typically trade in a single session and close all open trades at the end of the day, leaving no position open for the next day. Swing traders are traders who hold their position open for the next session or overnight. A day trader can trade using a variety of time frames on technical charts. These time frames can range from one minute or less to five minutes; fifteen minutes; thirty minutes; forty-five minutes; one hour; four hours; and even weekly and monthly. If you're wondering how a day trader can use weekly or monthly charts, you should understand the difference between time frames. Day traders choose their trading style by examining the charts and determining which time frame is best for them. Every day, many day traders can spend hours in front of their computer screens. However, many day traders trade only part-time, are preoccupied with other jobs or work, and cannot devote much time to trading every day. In such cases, these traders can examine weekly or monthly charts to determine when to buy or sell a stock. They then patiently wait for that level to arrive and trade only at that level. There are numerous ways to set an alert to notify you when a price level has been reached.

The brokerage platforms provide SMS alerts to their clients about stock prices. Most charting software includes the ability to send alerts when a stock price level is reached. They save valuable time and money by trading in this manner, which they can use to pursue other money-making activities such as a regular job or doing other work.

There's one more. Scalping is a highly skilled type of day trading.

Because the day trader focuses on a short timeframe (such as one minute or a few seconds) and trades for small profits, this is also known as micro-trading. They keep the lot sizes large so that small profits can compound into large sums of money. Because the timeframe is so short, scalpers can trade multiple times throughout the day, sometimes as many as 20 to 50 times. However, this is a risky type of trading that necessitates extremely fine trading skills. Otherwise, it is possible to lose all of one's trading money in a single session. Buying and selling on the same day is also referred to as day trading. Day traders, on the other hand, have a longer time frame for keeping their positions open than scalpers.

This can take anywhere from a few minutes to several hours. The Internet is rife with articles that show glamorous images of day trading, leading you to believe that you can get rich quickly using this trading method. However, this trading method necessitates hard work, knowledge, razor-sharp focus, and extreme patience, not to mention a large sum of money to invest in the early stages. When day trading, you must be completely focused; you must not allow yourself to be distracted by other things. If you can afford to have this level of discipline and dedication, you will find that day trading is a good fit for you. Day trading is also known as intraday trading. This term provides a more precise definition of a day trader because it indicates that buying and selling occur within a single day. Day traders can branch out into other types of trading, such as momentum trading, positional trading, swing trading, and long-term trading. All of these trading styles are specializations, but they do not usually fall under the day trading category.